WHERE MARTYRS RISE

Snow Flakes Don't Fall

ALBERT M. JABARA

Where Martyrs Rise

Snowflakes

Don't Fall

By

Albert M. Jabara

January 2023

Mirath Publishing Inc.
Ottawa ⸸ Canada

Books by Albert M. Jabara:

- Born To Write, 1967 Marquardt Press
- The Sonnet Gate And The Poem Cell, 1974 October Gull
- A Life of Many Paths, 1983 Jerusalem Publishing
- Thoughts Fall Like Rain, 1984 Wisdom House
- Crime Scene Collection, 2007 Mirath
- Crime Scene Collection, (Arabic Translation), 2008 Mirath
- Crime Scene Transcripts: Who Terrorized First? 2008 Mirath
- Prophecy on Ice, 2012 Mirath
- Love Moments Don't Rust With Age, (reprint 2018) Mirath
- Romance with Death, (reprint 2018) Mirath
- The Paradise, ALLAH Downsized To A Womb, (re-written 2019) Mirath, 1st printing cancelled
- Where Martyrs Rise, Snowflakes Don't Fall, (1st printing cancelled, 2nd printing re-written 2021, Mirath
- Assadiq al-watan lughet al-Um (Arabic), 2013 Mirath, 2nd edition 2021 Mirath
- Intended Terror (Arabic), Mirath 2023
- Lest We Forget (Arabic), Mirath 2023
- A Story In Instanbul (Arabic), Mirath 2023

Acknowledgements

The publisher recognizes the wholehearted efforts
with thanks and appreciation to all the creative professionals:

Cover design adaptation
created by Ivan Bobojcov
a genius in his own right

Islamic images and pictures
by unknown creators to whom we extend
our thanks and gratitude

Yunus Nefi's portrait adaptation
Sasha Borodin

Blueprint proofreading
- Jackie Lefebvre
- Mariam Jabara

Page design
Mohammad Dayfallah

Broad creative and technical input
Mohammid Abdul Latif Jabara

A ton of gratitude and appreciation
to Imam Mohamad el-Hady Toure
for granting permission
to use his phenomenal recitation
of the famous hymn
"tel elbedru aleyna"
in the promotional video

TABLE OF CONTENTS

Library and Archives Canada Cataloguing in Publication

Jabara, Albert M., 1947-, author
Where martyrs rise, snowflakes don't fall / by Albert M. Jabara.

Poems.
"Second printing (rewritten totally)."
Previously published: 2014.
Issued in print and electronic formats.
ISBN 978-1-988017-13-6 (softcover).—
ISBN 978-1-988017-11-2 (hardcover).—
ISBN 978-1-988017-14-3 (PDF)

I. Title.

PS8569.A22W44 2018 C811'.54   C2018-904601-5
                               C2018-904602-3

IN MEMORY OF MY PARENTS
MOHAMMAD TAHA JABARA
AND SOUMAYIA FARHAT JABARA

وَلاَ تَحْسَبَنَّ الَّذِينَ قُتِلُواْ فِي سَبِيلِ اللّهِ أَمْوَاتًا بَلْ أَحْيَاء عِنْدَ رَبِّهِمْ يُرْزَقُونَ

SPECIAL RECOGNITION

Aljazeera aired the arrest of a disciple of justice by Israeli forces for speaking out against apartheid. The story of Frank Romano, a law professor, fell on me like a roof. Half of me froze after hearing the interview; the other half shattered. Leaders who take a neutral stand on the war, ripping the Middle East, can stop civilians' daily slaughtering but do nothing. The interview refreshed my deep scars during my sixty-three years of writing. The professor left a university position, family, and friends to be with all Palestinians subjected to harsh authoritarian treatment and reminded Israel "apartheid" never outlives victims. I knew his impeccable record on human rights through his books, articles, T.V. interviews and book signing events.

The Zionists robbed an entire country and carried out murder, expulsion, and starvation against civilians under occupation. Forty percent of thirteen million Palestinians represent refugees in the region; 60% constitute those under occupation and abroad: All refuse to lose the right to return to Palestine, the land of their forefathers and ancestors. Since 1948 Israeli soldiers have arrested, tortured and murdered Palestinians and demolished homes.

Torah Jews represent 30% of the population inside Israel and a similar ratio abroad. Approximately seven million recognize Palestine, not Israel. Palestinians and Torah Jews inside and outside occupied Palestine account for twenty million. That explains Israel's fears of the two-state solution. All Arab states, the European Union, North, Central and South America, Africa, and Asia, agreed to the two-state solution. Israel appears to go along with the remedy. Through the action, it continues confiscating land, killing, and arresting protesters. Israel turned Gaza into a prison, demolished thousands of homes, and stole half the West Bank and a substantial area of the eastern

وَلَا تَحْسَبَنَّ الَّذِينَ قُتِلُواْ فِي سَبِيلِ اللهِ أَمْوَاتًا بَلْ أَحْيَاء عِندَ رَبِّهِمْ يُرْزَقُونَ

part of el-Quds. With the latest geopolitical development, Arab dictators build bridges with the apartheid occupier and openly ignore Palestinians' rights.

Professor Romano's stand on the seven-decade (people without land) captured my heart. His position shook my mind and conscience; it fell on me as it touched all Palestinians and millions of others worldwide. Professor Romano's expressions on humanity (written and spoken) do not leave any room to juggle rights or wrongs. Narrowing the difference to settle severe crises like occupation or oppression cannot achieve complete justice. Only the Palestinians, the rightful owner of the land, can share the land as they already did with many Torah Jewish refugees who fled World Wars I and II and settled in Palestine and other Arab countries. They did not move into tents, nor were they prosecuted or mistreated. They started a new life on arrival.

Already a world figure, gainful poet, writer, and law professor who understands justice as natural justice is, not how others tailor it. I referred to the professor as "a disciple of justice," for I learned a new meaning of humanity from him. I cannot claim I have read all his books, articles, and poetry. But what I read analytically and digested carefully convinced me there exists between people, a relationship higher than blood connection. His words in the short interview struck like the light of gentle lightning. He reminded me of the miraculous story about Prophet Musa [pbuh] and the Pharaoh. Freedom won over oppression by the power of a staff that split the Red Sea. I felt we are two siblings in a soul.

Professor Romano shames the superpowers of nukes and missiles. He lobbies for peace; they incite a war to sell weapons. The professor shames wealthy Arabs who spend foolishly on forbidden cravings and ignore their people. According to Islam, if wealthy Arab Muslims paid Zakat, the world would not have one child, mother, adult or elder dying of starvation. The Holy Qur'an firmly expects the abled to pay the Zakat as it is a debt owed to needy people and people with low incomes. The Holy Book resolutely compels the abled to stop oppression and wars against the weak and the impoverished.

وَلاَ تَحْسَبَنَّ الَّذِينَ قُتِلُواْ فِي سَبِيلِ اللهِ أَمْوَاتًا بَلْ أَحْيَاء عِندَ رَبِّهِمْ يُرْزَقُونَ

Jane Fonda forced the U.S. Administration on its knees to accept peace with Vietnam. She lobbied against the war from university campuses and street corners in major cities. Three-quarters of Americans rallied behind her humanitarian campaign.

Professor Frank stands in the face of oppression and apartheid, unafraid of reprisal. The CREATOR designates high ranks for martyrs. The professor earned that status, and he is still among us.

I dedicate this book
to Professor Frank Romano
from the depth of my soul
and pulse of my heart.
I know
my humble recognition
only covers
a dot of a mountain of the burden he carries
to help the oppressed and stop injustice.
The professor taught me a lesson
worth a hundred honours.

وَلاَ تَحْسَبَنَّ الَّذِينَ قُتِلُواْ فِي سَبِيلِ اللهِ أَمْوَاتًا بَلْ أَحْيَاء عِندَ رَبِّهِمْ يُرْزَقُونَ

16

وَلاَ تَحْسَبَنَّ الَّذِينَ قُتِلُواْ فِي سَبِيلِ اللّهِ أَمْوَاتًا بَلْ أَحْيَاء عِندَ رَبِّهِمْ يُرْزَقُونَ

FOREWORD

Yunus Nef'i learned the brain could store a million trillion terabytes by today's standard. He studied the interaction of family, friends, neighbours, strangers, nature, animals, and little or large things that emboldened visions, including action and reaction, emotions, love, hate and envy. From an early age, he dreamt of becoming a medical scientist. He assigned his services exclusively to his body as the "patient" and played the "doctor." He prescribed the air in the village, mom's cooking, well water, wholesome fruit from dad's garden and ever-blooming love.

His ultimate dream was to find a cure to realign messed up chemicals in the body. When an army commander gives a prep talk to his soldiers before going to war, the body chemicals become disoriented instantly. Soldiers are not born killers; rapists are not born molesters; dictators are not born thieves or oppressors. Every newborn coming to this world falls into loving, caring hands, goes to earlier schooling, moves on to higher grades, walks away with a degree, or becomes a baby victim, victimized by parents, society, and the establishment.

Yunus Nef'i's theory suggests the inner doctor in our body understands, identifies, and assesses problems before applying the solution. On Monday morning, a co-worker surprised you with a mean slur in the presence of the other staff. You walked away torn, pride and dignity destroyed. Twenty-four hours later, a severe headache drove you insane. You rushed to the medicine cabinet and took painkillers. In truth, your internal doctor restored your pride and dignity and stopped the headache. A healthy, stable behaviour faces no risk of chemicals freaking out.

Also, harmful consumptions such as excessive sugar, salt, narcotics, tobacco, alcohol, and a longer list of bad diets, including ingredients found

وَلاَ تَحْسَبَنَّ الَّذِينَ قُتِلُواْ فِي سَبِيلِ اللهِ أَمْوَاتًا بَلْ أَحْيَاء عِندَ رَبِّهِمْ يُرْزَقُونَ

in every medicine available off the shelf or prescribed, lead to a psychotic state.

Anyone can turn moral obligation 360 degrees by exposing bad parents, teachers, governments, and religious apostles. Exploring the gift of life in all facets leads you to your internal doctor, through which you discover a virtual clinic not far from the forebrain, the midbrain, and the hindbrain. The seamless doctor is an automated system in a sealed brain sector. People cannot sense it in action but feel it by reading the mood, the frustration, and the relief.

Yunus Nef'i believes a natural science exists inside the body but is not recognized. People use one-tenth of the brain; the rest is not under a mountain. A heart sustains an ocean of mercy, pumps blood to every tissue, organ, vein, muscle, flesh, bone, and skin, never tires, and stops when life ends. The heart rules the five senses that serve the body. The brain archives a million times more than the Library of Congress.

Study your body thirty minutes a day, discover your internal doctor, explore your natural science, decide who you are, bring out the buried potentials that can benefit you and others. Every good you do for a fee or free renews your budding like a fruit tree.

The irony in Yunus Nef'i's dream is that he did not become a medical scientist. The doctor he played was the poet his soul conceived, carried, and delivered. His study yielded a pyramid of metaphors. A word, and a line, building up to a book of each of his works (during seventy-five years of writing), earned him a scientist's sense: Poetry the patient and pen the cure. His heart functioned as the inner doctor; poetry gave him inner peace; the poet in him controlled his life. Perhaps Mariam, a few years after completing her medical science degree, will carry his medical scientist dream and turn it into a reality. The youngest of his four children loves Papa's poetry and stories. Papa once asked her if she had finished reading his last book. She replied, "I would have if I could turn off the tap of my tears."

Mariam dabbles in poetry occasionally and comes up with beautiful metaphors. Poetry invaded her fancy until her father convinced her to stick

وَلاَ تَحْسَبَنَّ الَّذِينَ قُتِلُواْ فِي سَبِيلِ اللّه أَمْوَاتًا بَلْ أَحْيَاء عِندَ رَبِّهِمْ يُرْزَقُونَ

to medical science, write poetry in her spare time and stay close to his new work. She inspires his poetry with her tender heart and crystal thoughts. Both could be sitting in the family room; he talks about his parents and the village; she lends her ears to each word. These moments brought back memories of the garden he routinely visited in the early morning, stuffed himself with black and green figs. At the same time, the cool breeze fanned his hair over his back and face.

He reads a dua'a during prayer for his deceased grandparents, parents, and siblings. He asks ALLAH to protect his children, grandchildren, loved ones and friends. As he folds his mat, an image sweeps his eyes. Above him floats a single cloud not far from his head; Mom stands by the woodstove cooking; Dad walks in with a fruit basket. Yunus Nef'i considers himself blessed with super imagination, which allows him to recall the past and relive the moments as they once existed.

Obsessed with snow, he never saw or touched it. Engulfed in poetry, he wrote little of it. Every world conflict saddened and confused him. Civilized and dictatorship regimes alike waged wars and killed innocent people. These obsessions lingered on for seventy-five years. Every day, his emotions rose and dipped like the temperature.

Yunus was born and raised in Yemen's el-Hutaib village, which stands over ten thousand feet above sea level. Clouds float at eight-thousand feet. el-Hutaib, it has never had the joy of receiving rain or snow. His grandmother, born in Lebanon, told him many breathtaking stories about rain and snow. Every time he looked down at the clouds two thousand feet from his window, a craving arose: He pictured himself touching and playing with the flakes. Only men could descend the valley and experience the generosity of the clouds.

Turmoil in the Middle East confused the ten-year-old. He packed his memories of his village, home, and school friends three years later. He and his family landed at the Port of Montreal on November 18, 1944. He played in the snow during the few days they stayed with relatives. They settled in Ottawa; he worked casually to help the family with rent and food.

وَلاَ تَحْسَبَنَّ الَّذِينَ قُتِلُواْ فِي سَبِيلِ اللهِ أَمْوَاتًا بَلْ أَحْيَاء عِندَ رَبِّهِمْ يُرْزَقُونَ

Yunus Nef'i travels on foot, by train, air, and sea. But when his mind moves, the journey stops the time. Young boy to age ninety defends his theory: Humans connect physically and spiritually. A thin line separates the two: Each yields a unique experience; one, we consume; the other, we absorb mentally.

Realism and abstraction make one body of two shades. Yunus Nef'i knows how close authenticity is to the obscure. He fell in love with snow he never saw in his village. When he arrived in Canada and physically touched the flakes, he sensed the exact feeling in his grandmother's stories about snow in Lebanon, the country of her birth and upbringing.

The political novel stages the first human murder and then moves to 1088. Pope Urban II approved Muslim civilians' killing and destroying life sources, properties, homes, and buildings.

The novel's blend of war, journalism and poetry presents a fresh experience, rare in style and diction. Metaphors, meticulously crafted, you do not find in English literature from Beowulf's days, the poet, to the present day. Soulful love episodes pop up startlingly. The soothing solace intimately strikes, lacing the heart with a breeze of oxygen. Even though the lines bleed on the page and ache the chest and soul, the brain slowly absorbs his thoughts like a delicious meal you want to last longer. Grief, anger, and the world's shame dominate the novel, but not short of roses, flowers, love stories and wedding bells.

وَلاَ تَحْسَبَنَّ الَّذِينَ قُتِلُواْ فِي سَبِيلِ اللهِ أَمْوَاتًا بَلْ أَحْيَاء عِندَ رَبِّهِمْ يُرْزَقُونَ

CHAPTER ONE

Where martyrs rise, snowflakes do not fall. You cannot see clouds or hear hurricanes, storms, or rain. Everything under the soil and above it, including all within the highest skies to lowest oceans' floors, motionless hold as Liele'et el-Qadr. The air opens zillion eyes to ensure nothing moves when martyrs rise.

Martyrs rise in graves. No one knows when and how they ascend. What Yunus Nef'i cannot see, touch, or feel, he imagines pen in hand and a metaphor on the tip of his tongue. But martyrs rise (alive) in white columns to the Eternal World.

No humans saw them ascend. ALLAH says they do rise. Can any person or creation doubt the Word of Allah?

> They rise through the sky;
> thoughts spire with them;
> they perfume the Universe;
> hands cannot fly
> but feel the musk
> and pass it on to lips.
>
> Eyes surf the space;
> gravity clears the way.
>
> Martyrs rise in holy shrouds;
> angels stand at Heaven's doors
> and welcome the comrades
> to new homes.

وَلاَ تَحْسَبَنَّ الَّذِينَ قُتِلُواْ فِي سَبِيلِ اللّهِ أَمْوَاتًا بَلْ أَحْيَاء عِندَ رَبِّهِمْ يُرْزَقُونَ

Seventy seconds end the journey;
Yunus Nef'i's eyes and heart
store the scenes
inside his memory.

ALLAH chooses martyrs before conception or after holy mothers deliver them. Martyrdom embodies the most profound miracle and least understood. Martyrs may not accomplish the whole desired mission in the first bout. If ALLAH wills, they return countless times soldiers in lit form. Oppressive empires fall and perish, not by any mighty human power. The Holy Qur'an states clearly: ALLAH's Soldiers exist on the Earth and in the skies.

Martyrs (soldiers of a unique type among various creations) assisted human fighters small in numbers against armies a thousand times larger, armed with highly advanced weapons.

Martyrdom is the core of faith, power-driven by Shadow Energy, identical to the sun's force, the moon, lightning, tornado, storm and hurricane. World nukes, military forces of America, Russia, China, India, Israel, and the wealth of Arab dictators will not last five seconds against positive lightning or less thereof.

Yunus Nef'i imagines the Universe as a giant clock. The martyrs' journey begins; the ticking stops. A bright path opens; fig and olive trees, side-by-side lower branches remain in Salam until martyrs reach the doorsteps of Heaven.

ALLAH shows them the Higher Paradise at the very second of martyrdom so they do not feel like strangers when arriving at their new home. Immortally they rise and descend; notably, they live and fight—martyrs born once never die. The best definition of a martyr is a soldier fighting dictators and oppressors and a protector of truth and justice.

These verses confirm that Islam does not permit deceased prayer on martyrs. "And say not that those slain in the cause of ALLAH are dead. Nay, they are alive, but you perceive it not" (2):154 Qur'an. "Think not that

ولا تَحْسَبَنَّ الَّذِينَ قُتِلُواْ فِي سَبِيلِ اللهِ أَمْوَاتًا بَلْ أَحْيَاء عِندَ رَبِّهِمْ يُرْزَقُونَ

those killed in the way of ALLAH are dead. Nay, they are alive, with their LORD, and they have provision" (3): 169 Qur'an.

"They rejoice in what ALLAH has bestowed upon them of His Bounty and rejoice for the sake of those who have not joined them but are left behind (not yet martyred)—that on them no fear shall come, nor shall they grieve" (3) 170 Qur'an. "They rejoice in Grace, and Bounty from ALLAH and that ALLAH will not deny the reward of the believers" (3):171Qur'an.

Martyrs do not die; we perceive them dead; they join the angels, ascend to Heaven, and descend to Earth when duty calls. As messengers, they return in human form, as holy soldiers descend in Shadow Energy not visible to the enemy. ALLAH also grants martyrdom to helpless civilians of all ages, including unborn infants who die during vicious war, assassination, or hate crime and those who die of grief beyond control.

ALLAH grants martyrdom to the one upholding the pen and the voice of justice, truth, honour, and the land. Grants martyrdom to the one who applies the Holy Qur'an and teaches the learned, illiterate, scientist, and ignorant. Also, ALLAH grants martyrdom to one who teaches the poor how to earn a living—and the rich who seeks the have-nots to give generously.

Martyred pregnant mothers give birth in Heaven; martyred elders water and groom gardens in the Seventh Paradise; each infant and child brattled by F-16 or killed by a bullet earn four wings, a light life and an abode in Paradise. Miriam in hijab, fifty worshipers in Christchurch mosques, Jamal and all before them pray freely in Heaven while killers roast in Hell. Children who die of horrific sorrow over the loss of parents join mom and dad at a dinner table full of food, fruit and ZamZam water.

Before martyrs rise, a pathway opens. All that rotates freezes: Air stops floating and flowing; winds, storms, and tornados deflate and disappear; oceans subdue hurricanes; the Earth suppresses volcanos; clouds migrate to a place of a distance equal to one-tenth of a tenth of a billion ly.

The eyes of the air guide martyrs to their destination as they rise. Each gate of the Seven Skies opens a rose-shaped door as martyrs enter or depart.

ولاَ تَحْسَبَنَّ الَّذِينَ قُتِلُواْ فِي سَبِيلِ اللهِ أَمْوَاتًا بَلْ أَحْيَاء عِندَ رَبِّهِمْ يُرْزَقُونَ

Martyrs rise where snowflakes do not fall for reasons we do not know and are not privy to know.

Snowflakes also become martyrs when they melt, giving life to future offspring of all creations. They sanitize and perfume the skies, fall to kill pollution in the air and on the ground; earn martyrdom when they dissolve. Thoughts of integrity and purity also become martyrs when ascending in generations' minds and immortally remain on the page.

Snowflakes and human martyrs belong to the Shadow Energy group in holy power and unlimited blessing from ALLAH. Literature falling into untrustworthy hands prevents martyrdom. For that reason, we find fewer committed poets and authors dedicating all their work to the truth and nothing but the truth—often referred to as seers.

In this book, martyrdom appears sad. It is the holiest and most noble deed. Habeil died by his brother's stone knife. On that tragic day, martyrdom became the supernatural and immortal force against oppression, injustice, and forgery. ALLAH granted martyrs the highest status over all human beings; every person, including prophets, lives and dies. Martyrs do not die.

Iblis tricked Adam and Hawa thirteen thousand years ago when he made them strip naked in a garden. Iblis scored a little victory but lost his place in Paradise. Adam and Hawa descended to the Earth; their species split: Son Habeil followed the truth; Gabeil went astray and refused redirection.

Heaven's copper sand covered Adam's feet to the waist for forty years; ALLAH sent the soul a few grams of air. Adam breathed, opened his eyes, and screamed a long, loud cry.

Blood rushed into his veins and powered his heart. Adam walked, scooped water with both hands, drank, did wudu and prayed. ALLAH asked the angels to kneel before Adam; Iblis refused and protested, "Creation of fire cannot kneel before a person of clay."

(In the Heaven),
Adam slept
under olive and pomegranate trees

وَلاَ تَحْسَبَنَّ الَّذِينَ قُتِلُواْ فِي سَبِيلِ اللهِ أَمْوَاتًا بَلْ أَحْيَاء عِندَ رَبِّهِمْ يُرْزَقُونَ

for three Fajrs,
his rib parched,
a sun dropped
golden ray on his shoulders,
a moon breathed in his eyes,
clouds rained on his face,
Hawa popped from his rib:
She picked black and green olives
and placed them in his hands,
peeled the skin of a pomegranate
and gave him the arils.

(In the Earth),
Adam's rib shivered
as Hawa walked, breathed,
smiled, or cried - - he felt
half his heart dropped to the ground:
Gabeil at the hills of el-Hutaib village
with a stone knife in hand,
Habeil stared at his fiery eyes,
Gabeil killed his brother:
Since that murder,
killing spread long and wide:
Forensic doctors need an ocean of ink,
the Amazon Forest
and a paper mill fifty miles long
to document all the crimes.

Yunus Nef'i stepped on the road of humanity that started in Adam's home. Habeil, the wise and pious; Gabeil, the jealous genius, each offered the LORD favour. The LORD accepted Habeil's, rejected Gabeil's. Gabeil's jealousy, envy, and burning hatred caused him to kill his brother because he could not control his jealousy, which turned him into a malicious Zionist.

If Hawa knew Gabeil would turn into a Zionist murderer, she would have strangled him at birth. Habeil wore a martyrdom crown and ascended to

وَلَا تَحْسَبَنَّ الَّذِينَ قُتِلُواْ فِي سَبِيلِ اللهِ أَمْوَاتًا بَلْ أَحْيَاء عِندَ رَبِّهِمْ يُرْزَقُونَ

Heaven. Gabeil still roasts in Hell agelessly and deathlessly. The Earth got her first martyr; Heaven opened all doors and welcomed Habeil. The angels gained a new comrade. Habeil commands an army of martyrs in Heaven; Gabeil and killers bounce into Hell, roast in boiling fire, and immortally burn.

For thousands of years, researchers, criminologists, scientists, and psychologists considered Gabeil's crime isolated and incidental; they accepted envy and jealousy as a natural and typical human reaction. Maybe so, but not when it leads to crimes and murders.

U.S. and European leaders share the scientific analysis and reject that Gabeil's crime matches all the sins and atrocities of modern-day Zionists. But do not dispute the earlier Crusades' wars against Islam in 1088 and continued to the present day, had started by a sibling of a Zionist of Iblis species.

Killers, murderers, and oppressors believe the people they killed gave them victory. Do they know Hell awaits them with arms of flames and bosoms of fire? Do they know they carry the genetic line of Gabeil that shall taint the blood of their children and grandchildren and continue contaminating them forever? On the scale of humanity, hair weighs more than them. Victims enter Heaven; they forever get all they desire good living, peace, and love.

Dictators, oppressors and murderers live in a shell without honest hearts and souls. Leaders who order the killing and those who carry it do not understand this perfect justice. But if they do, they will not miss a prayer, fast throughout Ramadan, pay Zakat, and fulfill Mecca's pilgrimage.

Tyrannical empires of the past crashed one after the other; martyrs earned immortality—survivors gained a raincheck. America's crash is inevitable; the USSR shattered like glass. Russia survived but cracked socially and morally. U.K. and France, aged down in power, cannot rise from their callous past. Asperity, venom and hostility against Muslims devalue China and India. ALLAH's punishment could sweep dictators and bigots in a small tissue or throw them into an ocean of wrath.

وَلاَ تَحْسَبَنَّ الَّذِينَ قُتِلُواْ فِي سَبِيلِ اللهِ أَمْوَاتًا بَلْ أَحْيَاء عِندَ رَبِّهِمْ يُرْزَقُونَ

Whatever punishment befalls: Dictators and bigots go to the lower chambers of Hell; burn agelessly and deathlessly. Islam moves forward; abominable countries rise but inevitably fall and crash on landing.

The conspiracy of Trinity faded a century ago. Christianity lost 75% of its populous followers. Truth-seekers exposed those who created ISIS and PKK and confirmed the founders are Farsi-Iran, Israel, Christian Evangelists, remnants of the Old Crusades, and Arab dictators.

ALLAH hears all, sees all; advances or forwards punishment as HE sees fit. If HE wills, a tod can tow the largest fleet, and a bee can hold down B-52. If HE wills, a snowflake or a drop of rain can destroy all nukes. If HE wants, a spider or an ant can blind soldiers, block ears, and freeze tongues and teeth.

Malicious flaws turn into warped judgment, a tool for aggressors and killers. The wrongs repeated, recapitulated enough times, become mores and norms.

Deformed leaders of poor and rich nations, superpowers, or underdogs, apply these malicious flaws to murder, invade, rob, and destroy. These flaws settle inside the bone structure of society; human emotions turn into black rocks. Thinkers and sociologists, who write and speak about human evolution, omit the species' hypocritical side but focus on modernization, which provides many means of comfort.

Travel distance is shortened to a fraction in comparison with life before. Plenty of food and water became available with little effort; science explored the Earth's four corners. Scientists created robots with emotion and compassion but failed to hold back bigotry, hatred, war, and discrimination.

In 1088, Pope Urban II intended to destroy Islam at any cost. He introduced a mindless, heartless decree that surpassed the most savage wars and battles after Gabeil's murder-crime of thirteen thousand years ago. The Pope raised racial and religious tension by his decree, which allowed the destruction of the life of all forms around Islam and Muslims, including other people of tolerance toward other faiths.

وَلاَ تَحْسَبَنَّ الَّذِينَ قُتِلُواْ فِي سَبِيلِ اللهِ أَمْوَاتًا بَلْ أَحْيَاء عِندَ رَبِّهِمْ يُرْزَقُونَ

Iblis did not hold such hatred against Adam and Hawa. The Pope, not Iblis, had to be the One-Eyed Lucifer's twin brother, who now lives on an island that harbours Iblis species and breeds baby Satan.

The evil breed appeared in past empires such as the Romans, the Farsi, the Mongols, Spain, Russia, Great Britain, France, and the Crusades. Modern-day democracy of most Western and other governments applies some form of justice internally. Still, outside borders meddle and spread conflicts between people using religious or ethnic differences as the cause. The countries leading to tyranny or rule in two faces are China, India, Russia, most of Europe, the U.S., Farsi-Iran, Israel, and the other Gulf States.

The most vicious offspring are the Zionists and the Mullahs of Farsi-Iran. Listen to these verses, one in the voice of Iblis and the other of ALLAH's: "I will come to them from before them, and from behind them, from their right, and their left and YOU will find that most of them are unappreciative" (7): 17 Qur'an.

"You may entice them with your voice and mobilize all your forces and all your men against them, and share in their money and children, and promise them anything: The devil's promises are no more than an illusion" (17): 64 Qur'an.

The first verse tells us an army of the Jinn under the command of Iblis controls and motivates evildoers to spread wars, corruption, thefts, and murder. Simultaneously, the second holy verse breaks the news of a victory; despite destroying lives and other things, the devil's promises are no more than an illusion. The analogy from both verses identifies justice as not humanely enforceable for lack of honesty and sincerity. The precise intake, evildoers end up in Hell immortally punished deathlessly. Victims go straight to Heaven and live immortally in peace and tranquillity with everything they desire comes to them.

The material of the value unjustly destroyed returns directly from the offender's assets to the victim. If we follow the victim, we could see the results—and say: ALLAH venged on behalf of the victim.

The first life is a period of ninety-nine chapters; the audience sees you, but you do not see it. You lead the players or join them or follow the leader.

وَلاَ تَحْسَبَنَّ الَّذِينَ قُتِلُواْ فِي سَبِيلِ اللهِ أَمْوَاتًا بَلْ أَحْيَاء عِندَ رَبِّهِمْ يُرْزَقُونَ

Periodically and momentarily, the moving stage stops—time docs your performance.

Chapter one hundred begins and ends with you on this planet. You begin an immortal life in the Hereafter. Your deeds decide the place and the neighbourhood.

وَلَا تَحْسَبَنَّ الَّذِينَ قُتِلُوا فِي سَبِيلِ اللهِ أَمْوَاتًا بَلْ أَحْيَاءٌ عِنْدَ رَبِّهِمْ يُرْزَقُونَ

دُعَاءُ السَّيِّدَةِ عَائِشَةَ رَضِيَ اللَّهُ عَنْهَا

[يَا سَابِغَ النِّعَمِ وَيَا دَافِعَ النِّقَمِ وَيَا فَارِجَ الْغُمَمِ وَيَا كَاشِفَ الظُّلَمِ وَيَا أَعْدَلَ مَنْ حَكَمَ وَيَا حَسِيبَ مَنْ ظَلَمَ وَيَا وَلِيَّ مَنْ ظُلِمَ وَيَا أَوَّلًا بِلَا بِدَايَةٍ وَيَا آخِرًا بِلَا نِهَايَةٍ وَيَا مَنْ لَهُ اسْمٌ بِلَا كُنْيَةٍ اجْعَلْ لِي مِنْ أَمْرِي فَرَجًا وَمَخْرَجًا] "ثَلَاثًا"

وَلاَ تَحْسَبَنَّ الَّذِينَ قُتِلُواْ فِي سَبِيلِ اللّهِ أَمْوَاتًا بَلْ أَحْيَاء عِندَ رَبِّهِمْ يُرْزَقُونَ

CHAPTER TWO

Snowflakes clothed in a mist of pure musk; perfume the galaxy before reaching the Earth; provide many other feats we are not privy to know. Yunus Nef'i does not intend to prejudice the rain. Flakes are the babies of rain. If snow does not renew itself, we have no flakes, martyrs or poets breeding poetry and bridging the invisible with the perceptible. Yunus explains his perception of the little white saints in a poem:

Little white saints
cascade all that is hard or soft
including the pores of the air;
feed rivers and quench the land;
fill lakes, oceans and do more:
Bring joy to children
and brighten the world,
melt to save a life in seed or bud form.

From the second they fall
earn martyrdom;
each grain of soil receives
a flake to sanitize it of all harm.

Mountains above and below absorb them
and turn them into springs;
springs grow into rivers;
rivers become oceans - -
life cannot exist without snow.

Little white saints
speak of integrity, nativity
and thrumming,

وَلاَ تَحْسَبَنَّ الَّذِينَ قُتِلُواْ فِي سَبِيلِ اللهِ أَمْوَاتًا بَلْ أَحْيَاء عِندَ رَبِّهِمْ يُرْزَقُونَ

recite poetry as they fall,
children listen and dance; poets write songs.

Little white saints
sprinkle diamond dust
to moisten the air and slip through
the pores of the sacred clouds:
Arabic is the language of snow,
a flake's soul, brain, and heart,
and tashkeels are her scale:
A flake consists of seven crusts,
each crust displays
a poem in cursive Arabic,
a flake under a microscope
displays Arabic letters,
the jewels transform into a voice,
speaks Arabic, Anatolian,
Yiddish, English, French,
Spanish, Chinese and more.

The alphabet gave birth to music, calligraphy, and art. Music is the mother of poetry. Calligraphy opened the path to painting and sculpture: all provide the most sacred feasts for the mind, heart, and soul. Prophet Idris pbuh, founding father of the alphabet, wrote the first line; Arabic bloomed and never stopped budding. ALLAH chose Arabic because the recitation of the Holy Qur'an demands her scales and tashkeels. The language imprisoned Yunus Nef'i early on. He wrote short poems and stories after he and his small family moved to Canada. He assigned his heart to every word he wrote: the tashkeels were the voice; the white saints were the song; his lungs pumped air, and pen and paper sat on the windowsill behind his Lazy Boy desk.

After nearly three-quarters of a century, Yunus Nef'i discovered a clear connection between martyrs, snowflakes, and Liele'et el-Qadr, a Night ALLAH showered with blessings and bounties. Zillions of stars float; some

وَلاَ تَحْسَبَنَّ الَّذِينَ قُتِلُواْ فِي سَبِيلِ الله أَمْوَاتًا بَلْ أَحْيَاء عِند رَبِّهِمْ يُرْزَقُون

rotate; others stay still like a ball of osmium. Eyes of air and the irises of the Universe monitor all movements—all hold still on the Night of Nights.

He wheels his eyes between trees and the sky every Ramadan night. He watches the Vigilant Eye merging with the air, touching all that breathe until dawn's ambers leave, until trees, moon, and stars sleep, and the sky and clouds freeze in place.

"Verily, ALLAH sent the Holy Qur'an down on the Night of al-Qadr (Decree). And what will make you know the night of al-Qadr (Decree)? The night of al-Qadr is better than a thousand months. Therein descend the angels and the Ruh (Jibra'eel pbut) by ALLAH's Permission with all Decrees. Peace upon all that night until the appearance of dawn" (97): 1-5 Qur'an. Yunus reflects on what he saw on the Night of Nights:

On that Night, the leaves the catnap
on the elbows of branches,
air shuts all pores; rivers freeze the flow,
lakes hold still like a cemetery,
oceans calibrate all surfaces,
all sleep like crystal floor,
everything in a milky way
from the gigantic orb
to the smallest meteoroid
obeys silence until dawn:
The One Night is better than
Thirty-one thousand nights:
Jibra'eel and Angels pbut
descend and stay in the company
of the Earth until Fajr - -
glory to those who fast,
pay Zakat, pray and wish no
ills and harms to others:
beholders of the One Night
receive new faith,
those fast all Ramadan

وَلاَ تَحْسَبَنَّ الَّذِينَ قُتِلُواْ فِي سَبِيلِ اللهِ أَمْوَاتًا بَلْ أَحْيَاء عِندَ رَبِّهِمْ يُرْزَقُونَ

receive new red blood cells
and lose all sins.

Yunus Nef'i's journey began in English. He finished his first English collection in 1963. With barely any literary direction, he let his instinct lead. He realized the limitation of the English language compared to Arabic. He divided his passion equally, structured in Arabic, and wrote in English. Arabic metaphors swept him in a storm every time he held his pen. Foreign tropes present enrichment to literature when Arabic is the guest. Many academic thinkers and scholars compare the generosity of the alphabet with the sun in size and ray.

Original literature passes many hurdles and ends up with a DNA identity. That does not suggest an imperative need for a second language to develop a unique niche in writing. Metaphors belong to a spiritual world irrespective of culture, race, faith, or era. Sincere authors and poets recognize this fact and fight hard to keep the DNA intact. Yunus Nef'i compares writing to a girl who does not want to look like any woman. No two creations are alike or exist in the most obscure abstract. All creations or formations of the soul, blood, rock or stone, valley or mountain, creek or river, lake, or sea, silent or breathing, abide by the law of a spiritual world. Writing reflects on the living, the lifeless, and the unknown. Yunus echoes his love for the Arabic language in a poem:

Twenty-eight noble jewels
intercept the pupils of the eyes
and capture hearts - -
a letter, a stroke of a brush,
a word on a line, keynote in a voice,
metaphor in a symphony or chisel's shard brings
fortifications to souls:
poetry kneels at her feet,
calligraphists curve,
bend and flex her letters,
orchestra and voice follow her tashkeels
better than a maestro's baton.

وَلاَ تَحْسَبَنَّ الَّذِينَ قُتِلُواْ فِي سَبِيلِ اللّهِ أَمْوَاتًا بَلْ أَحْيَاء عِندَ رَبِّهِمْ يُرْزَقُونَ

There is no end to her domain:
Fifteen million words
meet loyal pens
and stir agile minds,
faithful pens place each word
in a perfect stitch,
readers
decorate and embroider
the metaphors
with thoughts and imagination
so lines do not shake
during reading.
The alphabet caresses the page
and crown the poem,
tunes the lines
and feed the reader's eye:
Building lines
and tuning metaphors
requires a levelled surface
and a scale - -
poets and authors of integrity
serve the holy language truthfully,
obey her commands,
freely swim in her vast oceans
and rise to brimming skies.

Yunus Nef'i waited for seventy years with a sore soul, unable to flirt with her metaphors or discover her origin. On the day he left the village as a boy, he promised her a date and dance that would begin after he toured her space and gathered enough of her beauty to fill a book. The romance started in 2016 "el-Hutaib 2000 Above the Clouds" was born from a yearning to touch the rain and to play in the snow. The book did not earn martyrdom, but Arabic readers witnessed the jihad to the last line.

English streamed into his life over Arabic, not out of mercy and compassion, but to ease his homesickness. The relationship lasted despite

وَلاَ تَحْسَبَنَّ الَّذِينَ قُتِلُواْ فِي سَبِيلِ اللهِ أَمْوَاتًا بَلْ أَحْيَاء عِندَ رَبِّهِمْ يُرْزَقُونَ

his disagreement with the English writing tradition and editors restricting the natural flow of words on a page. Editors and traditionalists chained literature in regulations. Art and music enjoy ample freedom: Creators freely employ brush, knife, string, or key. Emotions reform images or speak to the soul while the heart follows the beat. Yunus Nef'i had a flair for painting but retreated from that dream because of the material cost; pencil and paper cost a token sum.

His English teacher indulged in the first poem he wrote and wanted to make changes; friends, co-authors, and literary critics acted as consultants. The avid teacher's purpose and all taught him a valuable lesson. He reviewed his writing; tuned every line several times before consenting to publish. He raised his poems like a good mother. He knew poetry resides in a small galaxy that floats in a poet or writer's life like a baby inside a mother's womb. He cautions against meddlers claiming lordship of word structuring and levelling. Off-tune poetry or prose crashes not on the page but in minds after reading.

Yunus Nef'i is a poet who can write a phrase that bristles the hair on your skin and pulls emotion from the chest that makes soulful tears fall. Yunus Nef'i can build a story of flesh, blood, and bone, atmosphere the air metaphor the storm. Yunus Nef'i can write a compelling account of war crimes that can cause a dictator to fall. Yunus Nef'i can compose a hymn that can cause a nation's ground to dance under her people's feet and her flag freely to flutter. His mind and soul can fly to higher skies, pen in hand and eyes on martyrs as they rise.

Yunus Nef'i welcomes editors to catch silly spelling, tweak poor grammar and drop or add punctuations. Editors are the master guards of languages because they know how to utilize the sixth sense. He respects this giving and even admits it is the law.

But he will not allow editors to justify his line flow, reshape characters, diction, attire, or voice. Gifted editors create as writers and poets. Abusers on both sides spoil the gift of writing for selfish reasons.

The teacher and the friends ripped Yunus Nef'i's poem and suggested a reform, so metaphors remain mute. When he sensed emotions ripped and

وَلاَ تَحْسَبَنَّ الَّذِينَ قُتِلُواْ فِي سَبِيلِ اللّهِ أَمْوَاتًا بَلْ أَحْيَاء عِندَ رَبِّهِمْ يُرْزَقُونَ

heard the proposed changes, he and his metaphors successfully escaped the mercenary trap with a chance to earn martyrdom. The first poem, horrific experience and a young poet lost between free verse and rhyme, unclothed emotion and gave birth to metaphors. He maintained a beginner's attitude with each book up to age ninety.

Writing meant the world to him. He blocked egotism and fame from distorting his natural humbleness.

The writing flows from the soul and heart, not rocks. ALLAH accorded all creations, including literature, a chance to earn martyrdom. Yunus' metaphors might not destroy injustice and oppression, rescue mothers, children, and elders, but try to expose plots before they happen. Yunus does not believe in false alarms: He checks and sanitizes every word and line against the truth he learned well. In the world of martyrs, a trope displays its presence with trimmed ends and sides on pages that never fade.

The reader did not say it. Critics labelled Yunus Nef'i's writing as an "orphan disconnect of all English traditions." That gave him strength, not stress. He nourished and cared for his orphan for seventy-five years; he created metaphors as an artist mixes colours. His inner voice told the critics: "Eat your hearts out." He did not have issues; others wrote in the traditional format, but he would not do it utterly. Writing for him was and always will be a field he cultivates, decides the seeds, the theme, and the genre. Yunus, the baby poet, made the first step himself, memorized the beat, and walked.

He honours and cherishes poetry as a sacred vocation. He believes original writing possesses as much of a chance to earn martyrdom as martyrs and snowflakes. Writing begins as a small gift, develops, and evolves like the natural blessing of flakes.

Editors show no compromise - - justified right margin is the law. With much pride and joy, Yunus Nef'i defied that law. His debate is partly boisterous and hilarious, so editors do not take it for a stabber: Editors want the right margins justified and words lined up like soldiers in a ceremony. Editors do not understand the natural sacredness of line flow, and each word must stay where it falls. Defiance does not work when standards prevail.

وَلاَ تَحْسَبَنَّ الَّذِينَ قُتِلُواْ فِي سَبِيلِ اللهِ أَمْوَاتًا بَلْ أَحْيَاء عِندَ رَبِّهِمْ يُرْزَقُونَ

A manuscript that requires a shake, scissors, and pencil belongs to the trash; a poet or writer who consents to character surgery, new attire, diction, and voice should sweep floors. If editors change characters' dialogue, they may as well snip the writer's tongue and call it "editing."

Well-tuned fiction reads as poetic as the best of poetry. Editors can check spelling and grammar like a pharmacist filling a prescription - - no pharmacist can fill a prescription unless issued by a credited doctor certified in a practice license.

Editors do well for lazy politicians who expect a speech blasted with cosmetics and superficial flavours. They can refine graffiti and marketing blurbs; teach writing skills to a sales team and nasty boss. Editors can assist researchers in writing technical manuals, textbooks, newspapers, magazines, and operational and managerial booklets on emerging business writing. Editors are the best fit for evaluating new releases and the best fit to provide unbiased critiquing. Novices and pros wish for nothing more than an honest opinion. For at least a half dozen centuries, literature lost originality and became a commodity bought and sold. Most often, cheap literature reaches bookshelves while the gems remain buried.

Poets and authors carry a mission, refine and enhance thoughts, and turn them into breathing dialogue. Once the characters respond and reciprocate in the dialogue assigned to them, the writing masters achieve the goal. No poet, writer or editor has the right to butcher literature, replace metaphors with fake lines and suffocate creative writing.

Architects of prose and poetry have not yet passed the green level; ask editors to use scissors and knives, believing they will float one day. Cheating in writing is like an addiction; you cannot stop even if you become a saint.

Sincere poets and writers will continue to write as long as the sun rises from the east and the moon begins from a thin loop. Genuine editors, poets and authors adore literature like soil enjoys the rain like flowers produce different scents every new season to attract bees.

وَلاَ تَحْسَبَنَّ الَّذِينَ قُتِلُواْ فِي سَبِيلِ اللهِ أَمْوَاتًا بَلْ أَحْيَاء عِنْد رَبِّهِمْ يُرْزَقُونَ

Poems aren't a species, not bound by rules, urge poets to sacrifice all they got and weigh the satisfaction in the scale of true justice.

For poetry lovers, poems are roses and flowers. For hearts and souls is the oxygen. Poems cannot become babies by super stem cell incision. Poets clone life-knowing tropes never become mothers but can emanate a mom, a child, a tree, a leaf, a bee, an ant, a spider web, or a story of biblical times.

Poetry existed long before the sun, moon, and stars descended to the Earth with Adam and his wife.

The spirit of poetry, driven by Shadow Energy, travels in space and returns without warning, goes through purification before appearing in public unless hasty poets induce premature birth. After each occurrence, thoughts twist and roll, moods freeze, and tongue and brain numb; Yunus begins a new poem.

Poets mould metaphors of various images. Some resemble people, animals, roses, flowers, and anything nature holds in her palms; anything hides between her thighs. Every Godly creation to the course of air and water taught Yunus the art of reviewing and tuning. He transformed each completed work and labelled it "the next martyr." Martyrdom in writing means immortal life on the page. That does not come without a fight to the end.

Literature, for him, stands up (not stands out), one that speaks in an ethereal voice, connects with the reader one-to-one and reciprocates emotion and feeling. He drops a paragraph or a chapter if it does not fit his structure.

Yunus Nef'i learned great lessons from the Holy Qur'an. One verse describes the skies raised without pillars apparent to the eye; another verse refers to planets that float motionlessly, and others rotate. His favourite verses are on how ALLAH controls the Universe through a scale system, so each galaxy obeys the law of levelling, sitting still, or turning by calibration.

Yunus Nef'i prays forty times daily; a consistent image hangs in the air occasionally. Holy verses in a scroll unfold behind birds praying in a perfectly straight line, wings folded. He could not understand the holy verses or the miracle of birds in Salam, wings folded. He does not want to

وَلاَ تَحْسَبَنَّ الَّذِينَ قُتِلُواْ فِي سَبِيلِ اللّهِ أَمْوَاتًا بَلْ أَحْيَاء عِندَ رَبِّهِمْ يُرْزَقُونَ

question the reasons behind these miracles, fearing they will disappear. Once only, he thought the holy verses occurred because of martyrdom's passion and a burning thirst for snowflakes in the other seasons. Birds in worship, wings folded, carry a message he may never understand. He concludes his prayer in a salute, "Peace be upon you," pointing to the left shoulder first, then the right. The final tribute goes to angels, one on each shoulder. The devotion belongs to ALLAH. His dua'a favours families, neighbours, friends, loved ones, the poor and the oppressed, all prophets, companions and believers, and adds to the list as events unfold.

In closing, he asks for pardon for all the cravings that coaxed him to do wrong in times of weakness. Fajr's reading of the Holy Qur'an and praying forty times, twenty before dawn, cleanses Yunus Nef'i's inners from all the daily distortion and propaganda he contacts.

His new path led him to a society he never thought existed in the West. Thousands of Westerners brace Islam daily. Many great scholars, thinkers, and scientists interpret the Holy Qur'an more profoundly than Arab and Muslim scholars.

These truth-diggers collect everything written before and after the sixth century. They learned the Crusades burned hundreds of millions of Islamic books and archives but did not burn all the copies in Europe, Asia, Africa and the Middle East.

Arabs and other Muslims of different ethnicities failed to uphold Islam to the level it serves. West's truth-diggers will reconstruct the Islamic archives and reprint all related books to end Islamophobia. All right-wing movements that appeared during Pope Urban II's reign and continue into the twenty-first century will disappear.

These truth-diggers are not going to rewrite Islamic history. They will make the facts available to the general public and governments to draw honest, unbias conclusions about the holy religion and urge all humans worldwide to take the Holy Qur'an as the guide and reference for social, legal, and economic matters in private and public institutions centres.

وَلَا تَحْسَبَنَّ الَّذِينَ قُتِلُواْ فِي سَبِيلِ اللّهِ أَمْوَاتًا بَلْ أَحْيَاء عِندَ رَبِّهِمْ يُرْزَقُونَ

These truth-diggers came across the following holy verses, making them more determined to collect the records and reconstruct them correctly: "We do not send angels, but with the Truth, and then they would not be respited" (10): 8 Qur'an. "Verily, We ourself have sent down the Reminder (the Qur'an), and verily We, (Ourself) will be its Guardian" (15): 9 Qur'an. "Falsehood shall not come to it from before it or behind it" (41): 42 Qur'an.

وَلاَ تَحْسَبَنَّ الَّذِينَ قُتِلُواْ فِي سبيلِ اللهِ أَمْواتًا بَلْ أَحْياء عِندَ رَبِّهمْ يُرْزَقُونَ

42

ولاَ تَحْسَبَنَّ الَّذِينَ قُتِلُواْ فِي سَبِيلِ اللهِ أَمْوَاتًا بَلْ أَحْيَاء عِندَ رَبِّهِمْ يُرْزَقُونَ

CHAPTER THREE

Yunus Nef'i researched and hashed the story of 9/11 for two decades. Wars that followed gave him a riveting reason to purge anger and frustration that swelled his brain. He could not just extirpate his memory; he refused to use a recycle bin. He spread his anguish unto blank pages and loaded the printer with ink. 9/11 (intended or framed) killed three thousand innocent people. Homogeneous retaliation was not an eye for an eye but 2000 eyes. The price for 9/11 as of 2019 reached six million killed and injured of various ages, and thirty million lost homes, belongings, and properties. Countries of institutions turned into terrorist states. Financial loss soared to trillions of dollars.

Political analysts with rationed minds believe Bush Jr., the Neocons of the White House, and Israel planned 9/11. The U.S. Congress introduced a bill to pressure Saudi Arabia to compensate victims' families and avoid the courts. A public trial will certainly "spill the beans," convict Bush Jr., former senior cabinet members, Zionist chiefs, and Israeli officials. 9/11 achieved its objectives. Islamophobia peaked; not two Arab or Muslim countries saw eye to eye but broke the Muslim's brotherly bond; each became an enemy of the other.

Structural engineers confirmed the towers tumbled from strapped explosives to the foundations. A detonator triggered the blasts. The two crewless planes crashed into the two towers by a remote-control system. The U.S. maintains the tightest air-net space on Earth. Its sensor system and radars can spot an ant dragging its feet, a bee flying, or a shadow floating in midair. Osama Bin Ladin and his boys could not have pulled such a daring and highly engineered attack even if they had slipped through ground borders as shadows and left as shadows. The war on terror that proceeded exposed the plan and the plot of 9/11. The U.S. allies and others who hate

وَلَا تَحْسَبَنَّ الَّذِينَ قُتِلُواْ فِي سَبِيلِ اللهِ أَمْوَاتًا بَلْ أَحْيَاء عِندَ رَبِّهِمْ يُرْزَقُونَ

Arabs and Islam joined the retaliation directly or indirectly. The U.N., as usual, chose the closet. *The West took the Fifth Amendment.*

U.S. and U.K. invaded Afghanistan and Iraq. Farsi-Iran occupies four capitals. Putin scoops Damascus, and Israel demolishes Palestinian homes. America enforced the vexed law, which allowed proxies and enemies to kill mindlessly. The regime of Bashar, Farsi-Iran, Russia and China, Israel, Egypt, and India added pretextual law to their brutal security branches. On January 26, 2011, the Syrians conducted a peaceful uprising for six months. Bashar shelled them on the first day. *The West took the Fifth Amendment.*

Assisi slaughters innocent Sinai people around the clock after deposing Mursi and sending the elected president into a solitary prison. From July 3 to August 14, 2013, Assisi's forces raided opposition camps in Cairo, killing, injuring, and imprisoning tens of thousands and carrying atrocities throughout the year. Today he ordered the demolishing of mosques and homes. *The West took the Fifth Amendment.*

Farsi-Iran's militias buildup began after Khomeini appointed himself the Supreme leader in 1979. Khamenei, the present spiritual leader, posted four well-trained and equipped militia armies in four Arab countries and installed hundreds of sleeping cells worldwide. *The West took the Fifth Amendment.*

Mohammad Ben Selman lifted the law restricting women from driving a car and issued a decree allowing travel without the spouse's permission. He eased the rules on freedom of speech and tabooed culture. The freedom rendezvous did not last. Infiltrators, often called sleeping cells, spread like deadly cancer and fractured the historic bond dearly honoured by most Saudis. The infiltrators, on behalf of the U.S. and Israel, almost started a war between Saudi Arabia and the UAE against Qatar. *The West took the Fifth Amendment.*

Farsi-Iran's drug dealers and money laundering operations moved to Dubai, allied with International scammers who sold properties that never existed. International spy agencies rushed to Dubai, set up underground operations,

وَلاَ تَحْسَبَنَّ الَّذِينَ قُتِلُواْ فِي سَبِيلِ اللهِ أَمْوَاتًا بَلْ أَحْيَاء عِندَ رَبِّهِمْ يُرْزَقُونَ

and ignited conflicts, wars, and corruption. *The West took the Fifth Amendment.*

India suddenly cloned the ethnic cleansing program of Israel. It turned apartheid 360 degrees. Its Constitution granted Kashmir and Jammu a special status; Modi Narendra, India's new prime minister, abolished that right on August 5, 2019. Kashmir and Jammu face daily oppression. *The West took the fifth amendment.*

Israeli prime ministers, commanders and parliamentarians headed terrorist cells in the past. Their successors manage an army of terrorist settlers. No domestic or international court had touched the previous or present cell leaders. *The West took the fifth amendment.*

The Zionists terrorized London and Paris at the end of World War I and II, gave two ideologies, one born from the rib of Nazism and the other from the womb of Communism, and chose Capitalism as a guardian. *The West took the fifth amendment.*

Israel runs two states: Kill and starve Palestinians; the other provides settlers all the luxuries, special status, and licenses to kill without question or trial, denies Palestinians jobs inside the Green Line, and forces them to accept casual work Jewish Zionists refuse. Gaza's nearly two million population live in cluster camps sealed off from air, ground, and sea. F-16 fighters level homes; return and bomb after Palestinians rebuild. *The West took the fifth amendment.*

The Chinese military has arrested and tortured Uighurs since 1949 only because they are Muslims; guards rape women routinely. China possesses one of the darkest records of human rights abuse.

The Communist regime murdered millions of innocent people during the civil war. *The West took the fifth amendment.*

Putin destroyed three-quarters of Syria, killed, maimed, and expelled millions. Putin's ethnic cleansing against Grozny from 1994–1995 killed two hundred and fifty thousand civilians or half the city's population. The

وَلَا تَحْسَبَنَّ الَّذِينَ قُتِلُواْ فِي سَبِيلِ اللهِ أَمْوَاتًا بَلْ أَحْيَاء عِنْد رَبِّهِمْ يُرْزَقُونَ

USSR leaders killed tens of millions of innocent people during the civil war. *The West took the fifth amendment.*

The Arab Spring of 2011 awakened people heedless of colour and religion. The U.S., Europe and Farsi-Iran immediately created ISIS, PKK, and other militias. The founding fathers cleverly marketed the two groups as the most significant global threat. But behind doors, they directed the two terrorist groups to kill Sunnis in Iraq and Syria and bomb public places in Turkey. Arab and Western media participated in the conspiracy. Most world leaders digested the illusory scheme. *The West took the fifth amendment.*

Analysts who followed the tracks of ISIS saw the play-war between ISIS and Syrian soldiers, Militias of Iran, and even Russian troops. ISIS commanders disguised in Arabic attire and Arabic names came from Israel, France, and the U.K. Not one commander died or was injured. Obama reclassified PKK from a terrorist organization to an American militia and expanded the recruitment to include Kurds, Arabs, and Turkmen. PKK and Obama's coalition of forty countries played war with ISIS. Did a nerve in Obama's body twitch? No. Obama committed serious treason, and his two government branches showed no objection. *The West took the fifth amendment.*

Russia joined Obama's coalition and never entered any battle against ISIS. Farsi-Iran Mullahs cheered for Obama and his coalition. Obama and Putin protected Bashar from a fall and covered up his crimes and atrocities. Corrupt Arab and Western news inflated the ISIS threat against Syria and Iraq to the point that the hundreds of thousands killed, expelled, and jailed became old news. Bashar and Iran's militias became heroes.

The Arab Spring is like the night wanting to erase the day for good, but the day always rises, and the night follows behind. America's superpower, its proxies, Israel, Russia, and Farsi-Iran, will disappear before the Arab Spring disappears. Oppression suffers from short breath; Justice swims in the air; despotism never outlived justice in history.

Four new peaceful revolutions surfaced, and a repeat in Egypt. Sudanese and Algerian forced two dictators to resign. Victory will come once the old regimes become trashed withers. Iraqis and Lebanese promised a drive to

وَلاَ تَحْسَبَنَّ الَّذِينَ قُتِلُواْ فِي سَبِيلِ اللّهِ أَمْوَاتًا بَلْ أَحْيَاء عِندَ رَبِّهِمْ يُرْزَقُونَ

sweep all corrupt government officials and employees. Drive the Mullahs and militias of Farsi-Iran out of their countries; promised to hang Hassan, Beri, Michel, el-Maliki, and all the other leaders Faris-Iran installed.

Egypt's repeat happened in September 2019 and September 2020; the army blocked all roads leading to Cairo and arrested more than four thousand. Protesters moved to narrow streets of every district and region. Some used roofs and demanded the resignation of Assisi. Egyptians are known to put their anger on ice, but when it thaws, expect tremors and earthquakes.

Donald, Boris, Netanyahu, Vladimir, or Arab dictators cannot stop the Arab Spring's storm. Hundreds of millions still remember the 2011 uprising that began in Tunis and moved to Egypt, then Syria. Tunisians achieved essential goals; Egyptians were not so lucky. Syrians struggled the most and suffered the most.

Bashar invited Putin to his slaughterhouse in 2014. Russian fighter planes drop barrels of explosives daily. Eight million Syrians live in cheap tents in the Middle East under trees in a boiling climate or flooded ground. Millions also fled to Turkey, Europe, Asia, Africa, North, South, and Central America.

By the end of 2019, combined casualties killed, maimed, imprisoned, expelled, and not accounted for reached fifteen million or 60% of the population, 97% Sunnis. Bashar, the butcher, serves the interest of the West like his forebears.

Several hundred years ago, France offered Hafez's forebears to the southern region of Syria to rule under autonomy for the French occupation of the rest of the country.

The traitors agreed if the enclave became a French Province ruled by Alawite governor. At the end of 2019, Syrian casualties outnumbered World War I and II compared to conflict longevity, population and intended civilian killing. The Mullahs and Putin give a stupid reason for being in Syria. Say, they entered the war at the request of Bashar to fight ISIS and Syrian resistance fighters.

وَلاَ تَحْسَبَنَّ الَّذِينَ قُتِلُواْ فِي سَبِيلِ اللهِ أَمْوَاتًا بَلْ أَحْيَاء عِندَ رَبِّهِمْ يُرْزَقُونَ

Not one person or persons with a few marble believed ISIS threatened Syria, Iraq, America, Russia, Europe, Israel, or Farsi-Iran. 95% of the civilians killed by PKK, ISIS, and Obama's coalition, Farsi-Iran and militias proved Arab Sunnis were the target. The corridor Farsi-Iran used to ship arms to Bashar and Hezbollah was never interrupted. Obama and the coalition provided unlimited financial and military support to ISIS and PKK. Ten million Iraqis and fifteen million Syrians struggle daily as refugees or homeless.

Putin shamed his people and stripped them of their dignity. Ali Khamenei not only shamed his people but starved them. He presents himself as the deputy of ALLAH, lies like a Shaitan and tells the world his decree prohibits developing a nuclear weapon while his scientists work around the clock to make the bomb. His top generals, Soleimani and al-Muhandis, slaughtered thousands of Sunnis and bombed several European sites. On January 3, 2020, a United States drone strike killed the world's most wanted criminals near Baghdad International Airport.

The Houthis, the terrorist arm of Farsi-Iran, occupied Sana'a and other territories in 2014. By a mandate of the Yemeni government, Saudi Arabia and the UAE declared war against the Houthis. Yemeni civilians caught between the warriors paid a woeful cost: Killed and injured, death by hunger, and diseases crossed the threshold of a quarter million. How could the world forget? Yemeni sailors first walked on the soil of the Earth's four corners. Yemenis first introduced trade, farming, science and architecture. Their arts, poetry, and literature surpassed the elevation of the famous el-Hutaib village.

The Turks sheltered the Russians kicked out of North Europe a thousand years ago and provided food, water, and education. The Russians stabbed the Turks in the back and occupied their land (which is Russia today). In 862, they killed millions but did not stop there: They invaded the Central Asian Republics and forced oppression on the people. In 1912 the Republics had 26,000 mosques, by 1949, 415 mosques remained under KGB control.

Omar Ibn el Khattab introduced Islam to Farsi-Iran in 651 during his Caliphate, built schools, universities, and mosques throughout the country.

وَلاَ تَحْسَبَنَّ الَّذِينَ قُتِلُواْ فِي سَبِيلِ الله أَمْوَاتًا بَلْ أَحْيَاء عِندَ رَبِّهِمْ يُرْزَقُونَ

90% of Iranians embraced the holy religion and Sunni principles. In clarification of Sunnis, all siblings of Prophet Mohammad pbuh married Sunnis; his grandchildren married Sunnis. Companions and their siblings married Sunnis. Islam was one, is one today and will always be one. Sunni, a root from Sunnah, is not a sect but the Hadeeths Prophet Mohammad received through Jibrae'el pbut. Arabic became the language of Farsi-Iran. Scholars and thinkers used Arabic in all their research and writing for two hundred years.

Shi'ism surfaced after the death of the Prophet in 632. Farsi-Iran forced all citizens to embrace the cult. Abu Lulu al- Majousi, an enslaved Persian, assassinated Omar Ibn el- Khattab in a mosque under the Mullahs' order; they built a shrine in the enslaved person's name. The cult leaders prosecuted anyone using Arabic and shut down all mosques.

So true is the old saying: "If you bury the tail of a dog under a mountain for a thousand years, do not expect to find a straight tail after you remove the mountain." The Mullahs still use Islam to attract reverts to Shi'ism. One Ayatollah, after the other, proclaims himself a holy deputy of ALLAH.

Iranians secretly reject the deputy forgery; remain mute for the same reason not to leave Shi'ism out of fear of facing execution or hanging. Nearly all Shi'ite Arabs, Iranians or others living elsewhere reject the deputy forgery and refuse to visit the fake shrine of Abu Lulu al- Majousi.

وَلاَ تَحْسَبَنَّ الَّذِينَ قُتِلُواْ فِي سَبِيلِ اللهِ أَمْوَاتًا بَلْ أَحْيَاء عِندَ رَبِّهِمْ يُرْزَقُونَ

وَلاَ تَحْسَبَنَّ الَّذِينَ قُتِلُواْ فِي سَبِيلِ اللهِ أَمْوَاتًا بَلْ أَحْيَاء عِندَ رَبِّهِمْ يُرْزَقُونَ

CHAPTER FOUR

Islam forbids the killing of innocent unarmed people and the bombing of homes and public services in wars; forbids harm or destruction to all life sources; prohibits the abuse of tame and wild animals; prohibits detaining suspects without proof and torturing prisoners.

Pope Urban II took advantage of the strict Islamic codes. His decree in 1088 gave the Crusades the right to kill innocent Muslims to force the Ottoman Army to leave the Mediterranean, Eastern Europe, and Asia. The Pope knew only 5% of Muslims lived among 95% of Christians in Eastern Europe and 15% of other ethnicities in the other regions. After two hundred years of nine wars and thirty battles, they mindlessly bombed all neighbourhoods and districts. Killed and expelled millions and turned homes, properties, and all life sources to rubble and debris.

The satanic Pope played "god:" promised surviving soldiers a home and lifetime pension of gold and silver; those who die in action meet the Trinity. When, where, and how, the Pope did not say. The god of murder pledged to delete the sins of the dead and the survivors. When, where, and how, he did not know.

It took the Crusades a hundred years of preparation for the longest and deadliest war ever. Plotters penetrated nations that embraced Islam and countries that supported Ottoman rule, planted hatred seeds, and encouraged people of other faiths to rise against Ottomans and Islam. They recruited informers to training camps; graduates penetrated the establishment, served in the public and private sectors, and enlisted in the army. In each case, the traitors reached more than 15% of the local population. They collected the sensitive information and sent it to the Crusades' military command post. Ottomanphopia flourished. Undercover

ولاَ تَحْسَبَنَّ الَّذِينَ قُتِلُواْ فِي سَبِيلِ اللهِ أَمْوَاتًا بَلْ أَحْيَاء عِندَ رَبِّهِمْ يُرْزَقُونَ

Zionists bombed mosques, churches and Synagogues during worship and blamed the Ottomans.

Pope's decree caused over five-hundred million deaths and propagated criminals like Stalin, Lenin, Mao Zedong, and Hitler. Hawa, the mother of our species, admitted her son Gabeil was a Zionist. Any free-minded political scientist would tell you Zionism dropped its seeds in regions of crucial influence and fostered fascism, Communism, Capitalism, Crusadism and Shi'ism. Look at victimized countries, search deep into the cause of war, and measure the hatred and bigotry in a whole society of kin, skin, and culture. For example, the sectarian conflict in the Middle East saved no village, town, or city. Internal wars caused more grief and sorrow than wars between nations far apart.

If curious to track casualties, watch the minute arm on the clock, prepare a spreadsheet and input the number murdered, homes destroyed, buildings, and mosques, and include the millions of refugees. Western leaders are adamant about keeping the Arab Muslim world under their direction as their forebears did. The side effects of their actions tear a considerable chunk of the values egoistically boasted on every occasion—the family breakups and social decay, and domestic crimes continue on the rise to a level of no decline. What North America and Europe achieved in a hundred years could disappear if the mobsters' laws continue to dominate globally.

Arab dictators honeymoon with Trump and Netanyahu while Sunnis in Syrian, Iraq and Yemen lose children, parents, elders, men and women. Refugees run to any piece of land willing to shelter them. Obama honeymooned with the Mullahs of Farsi-Iran until his last day in office. The daily slaughtering of Palestinians never stops. Sunni Provinces in Iraq, Syria and Yemen turned into ghost land. Obama freed the hand of Russia and Shi'ite militias in four Arab countries. Putin dreamt of naval and ground bases in Syria, and Obama fulfilled his dream. Obama gave Israel the green light to build more settlements and promised a Palestinian state and peace in the Middle East in his famous speech in Egypt. He fooled leaders of conscience who thought of him as an honest leader, not jinxed by devilish politics.

وَلاَ تَحْسَبَنَّ الَّذِينَ قُتِلُواْ فِي سَبِيلِ اللهِ أَمْوَاتًا بَلْ أَحْيَاء عِندَ رَبِّهِمْ يُرْزَقُونَ

Victims' Families hoped the black American President of Muslim ancestry could sanitize America's image and apologize to the millions of orphans. The Shaitan played the twin devil: Clever one concealed the evils, and another presented righteousness. Before his presidency, America stood like a mountain, and Russia was a rock in a valley. He tumbled the reputation of the Pyramid. Putin's luck turned to gold; he walked away with the fake tough image and roared like a lion.

The Mullahs rewarded Putin's forces in Syria with the "Mutua Marriage," a prostitution permit ancient Farsi rulers introduced as a welcoming gift to returning soldiers from war. The Farsi Shi'ite cult still practices Mutua Marriage. Islam denounces the practice and classifies it as an unforgiven sin and "Fitnah" against women's honour and one of the more severe slanders. Fitnah is more extensive than murder. "Fitnah is worse than murder" (23) 192 Qur'an. "Whoever kills a person [unjustly]…it is as though he killed all human beings. And whoever saves a life, it is as though he saved all human beings" (5):32 Qur'an.

Obama knew America's power could have saved millions of Syrians, Iraqis, and Yemenis. His promises to the Syrian resistance fighters fell through like pouring water into a net. He knew Bashar's father attacked Hama's city on February 2, 1982, killing nearly forty-five thousand civilians within several weeks, jailing fifteen thousand and demolishing one-third of the beautiful city.

Obama massed PKK along Syria's northern border and armed them with anti-aircraft missiles and advanced weaponry to fight ISIS. His plan intended to shake Turkey's growth program and ingrain sectarian conflicts so the rising country returned to U.S. slavery. Trump urged PKK to ease off the bombing in Turkey and hold on to the gained territories. He changed Obama's plan in Syria from killing Syrians to confronting Bashar, Farsi-Iran's militias and Putin.

Fethullah Gulen, the Turkish traitor Obama harboured, almost triggered a war between Turkey and Russia. Turkey's ranking pilot shot down a Russian Sukhoi Su-24 in 2015. The conspiracy failed; 90% of the Turkish population rallied behind Erdogan.

وَلاَ تَحْسَبَنَّ الَّذِينَ قُتِلُواْ فِي سَبِيلِ اللهِ أَمْوَاتًا بَلْ أَحْيَاء عِندَ رَبِّهِمْ يُرْزَقُونَ

Erdogan's silent revolution wiped out illiteracy, poverty and national debt. Innovations in the military, education, scientific developments and farming climbed to 80% of domestic needs. These remarkable achievements only took twenty years. Two new turns added to Ottoman principles helped Erdogan to achieve his vision.

1- Today's generation has a significant advantage in competing for a superior attitude through God's best-giving EYE, the "Y5." People can decide if their inherited social norms are genuine or fake for the first time. They find answers to moral questions their leaders, clergies, and imams failed to provide.

2- Nationalism and ideologies nearly lost steam and posed no barb wires between people. Most people from all walks of life returned to a common tolerance era, respecting each other's culture and faith. The days of people following a shepherd or a dictator out of fear have disappeared except in China, India, Farsi-Iran, some Arab states and parts of Africa.

The Ottomans ruled three-quarters of the world for over six hundred years by the Holy Qur'an and the Sunnah principles of Prophet Mohammad pbuh. Erdogan builds bridges with other nations not to revive the Ottoman Empire. The empire already gave the world Islam, science, art, poetry, literature, architecture, mathematics, and medicine. It introduced the Aoughaff System. Aoughaff held "in-trust" everything, not deed purchased under the Shariah Laws. The Treasury of Aoughaff (known as Byat el-Mal) receives 20% of net revenues from Zakat at the year-end of the abled individuals and corporations.

Shariah Laws did not allow the leasing of Aoughaff; it did not permit state charges for healthcare, education, water, electricity, and fuel. Shariah Laws prohibited all forms of taxes against individuals and corporations. Recourse against crimes and all infringement on rights had no limitation periods. People experiencing poverty, orphans, divorcees, the old and people with disabilities received an adequate allowance to sustain a good life.

Annual budgets varied from one year to the next based on the economic condition. Aoughaff announced funding to all levels of governing, limiting

وَلاَ تَحْسَبَنَّ الَّذِينَ قُتِلُواْ فِي سَبِيلِ اللّه أَمْوَاتًا بَلْ أَحْيَاء عِند رَبِّهِمْ يُرْزَقُونَ

each level to 70 personnel. Only the Ministry of Defence operated under no limit in funding and personnel. Military personnel participated in the ministry's productive sector, planted and harvested necessities, and designed and manufactured household items. Aoughaff distributed food and other essential items to people experiencing poverty through Zakat. Literature, the arts, libraries and museums received 10% of the budget, and 25% went to public services and education.

Aoughaff legislated private corporations' earnings not to exceed 30% and limited 70 employees to each so others could start a business and pursue economic benefit. Turkey has not yet implemented all the holy Aoughaff principles, but not far from it. The Shariah rules are a long list that protects everything under the sky and all galaxies modern science accesses. Aoughaff operated independently as trustees with absolute power on behalf of the CREATOR. Governments operated as servants of the people and Aoughaff.

World scholars labelled the era "the Golden Age." Islam, nourished in the cradle of Arab wisdom, bloomed under the wings of the Ottoman Empire. Kurtoba's one monument of mosque, church and synagogue spoke volumes about Islam's just rule. People of the three faiths hugged and chatted as they left from three separate doors. According to the Holy Qur'an, only the level of justice and truth decides the ranks of people.

In twenty years, Turkey restored the Ottoman's infrastructure and turned it into a system run by institutions, debt-free to trading partners, including the World Bank. Tourism rises every year with surges in international trade and the economy. Turkey is the only country tourists exceed half the population. Erdogan's last word of wisdom to Europeans, Americans and all Arabs: "Pressure your leaders to repair or rebuild the family spine quickly. A society's spine is identical to a person's spine. Once the disks separate, the entire nation falls apart."

Turkey today mentors and assists over a hundred countries; it provides startup capital, expertise and know-how. Experts recognize the noble contender's surge technologically and scientifically against peers like the U.S., China, Germany, Japan, Russia, and South Korea. Erdogan

وَلاَ تَحْسَبَنَّ الَّذِينَ قُتِلُواْ فِي سَبِيلِ اللهِ أَمْوَاتًا بَلْ أَحْيَاء عِندَ رَبِّهِمْ يُرْزَقُونَ

successfully implemented a multi-ethnic governing system that protects all religions and ethnicities equally. Some argue Erdogan adopted the values of Western Democracy and left out the flaws. Others disagree and say the West inherited the Ottoman's charter of rights but left out any reference to Islam and the Holy Qur'an. Erdogan believes people worldwide prefer a weak system free of bribes over a fully-fledged democracy run by interest groups and thieves.

The U.S. population in 1915 was one hundred million, which grew considerably through the influx of immigrants. By 1967 it reached two hundred million. The growth slowed to three-hundred and fifty million in the twenty-first century.

Turkey today is where America was in 1915 but does not pursue war and occupation, steal resources or spread hatred among people. Turkey's fast-growing birth graph and immigration influx could put the population at two hundred million by 2050. The rising country is already an appealing infrastructure for brain and foreign investment. Turkey's gross national revenue could reach twenty-five trillion dollars before 2050, provided the U.S., Europe, and Arab dictators let the rising country be.

Turkish Cyprus and Turkey each have a share of the Mediterranean's Natural gas and oil resources as Italy, Greece, South Cyprus, Libya, Egypt, Palestine, Lebanon, Syria, and many others. Israel claimed Palestine's share as it unlawfully confiscated other land and properties. Assisi leased Egypt's share to Israel under a shady deal, free rent; the lease to lapse with the depletion of the resources. The dubious accord gives Israel 100% of the exploration and 100% of the share. On the other hand, Egypt must purchase all its oil and gas needs from its tenant at a marginally lower price but is not entitled to profit sharing.

Leaders of Europe threatened Turkey with sanctions. Erdogan ignored the threats and sent four exploration ships to The Mediterranean Sea. These leaders risk their people's beautiful life, scientific advancement, and wealth if all that would eliminate Islam, Mecca, el-Quds and Istanbul. The European Union's double standard against Turkey is not the first or the last. It began building a monetary system to bypass the U.S. sanctions against

وَلَا تَحْسَبَنَّ الَّذِينَ قُتِلُواْ فِي سَبِيلِ اللهِ أَمْوَاتَا بَلْ أَحْيَاء عِندَ رَبِّهِمْ يُرْزَقُونَ

Farsi-Iran, knowing the rogue regime participates in crimes against Sunnis in Iraq, Syria, and Yemen, including the bombing of public places in Europe.

Farsi-Iran is the exporter of terrorism globally. They recently bombed oil tankers owned by Gulf countries and seized a British liner in the Strait of Hormuz. On September14, 2019, Farsi Iran and affiliates attacked Aramco oil production plants. The attack shook the world economy. Trump turned his back to the Saudis. European leaders played the referee but favoured Farsi-Iran.

Tehran breeds deformed Mullahs. Khamenei, the self-ordained deputy of ALLAH baptizes future terrorists in pools of blood on Ashura day. Turkey must base its relationship with Iran on the pulse of the Arab masses and ignore the hatred of dictators toward Erdogan. Turkey should pressure Iran to stop oppressing and executing opposition. The mullahs hate Turks more than Arabs but are too scared to face the superior military force of Erdogan.

King Selman proposed to Erdogan an alliance of Arab and Muslim countries. Forty countries welcomed the plan. Trump thwarted the pact before it hatched. But thirty-six states stood by Turkey with the majority of their people.

Trump wants an Arab NATO in place to confront Iran. His goal is nothing but a lame horse, not of pure breed. Arab traitors cannot be warriors after being enslaved people for centuries. Trump and European leaders hunt in the same bunker to eliminate the Arab Spring but ignore Kameini's severe threat.

Only Turkey can secure stability in The Middle East, supported by 90% of Arabs and Muslims on Earth. Turkey carries five million Arab refugees; Arab traitors and infiltrators finance a defamation campaign against Erdogan and his government. The region needs Turkey, not Iran's Mullahs, welfare recipients like Israel, or a manipulator like Trump. Turkey controls one of Europe's most critical lifelines and provides crucial security for the ageing continent; it holds the second-most massive army in NATO. Turkey shows good faith; Europe reciprocates in conspiracies.

وَلاَ تَحْسَبَنَّ الَّذِينَ قُتِلُواْ فِي سَبِيلِ اللهِ أَمْوَاتًا بَلْ أَحْيَاء عِندَ رَبِّهِمْ يُرْزَقُونَ

In October 2019, the political climate turned 360 degrees in favour of Turkey's army moving into Syrian resistance fighters thirty-two kilometres into Bashar's northern borders. Trump found himself backed against the wall; he conceded to Turkey's demand for the non-militarized area and ordered Obama's mercenaries 100 hours to vacate all positions and hand over all heavy arms to the U.S. commanders.

Several coup d'etat attempts against Turkey failed, including on July 15, 2016. Print and digital smearing blitz paid by wealthy Zionists streamed through news pipelines in Europe and America. The war against the Turkish currency did not go beyond Wall Street. Citizens and businesspeople quickly converted all their U.S. dollars for liras at a profit. The lira rose; the dollar dipped.

Where would the world be today without the Ottomans? The Empire introduced every facet of learning, every path, and every discovery using the Holy Qur'an as the source.

The Holy Book is the comprehensive, Unabridged Guide narrated in part in ALLAH's Voice, stories told by Jibra'eel, Angels, prophets and Seers pbut. A surah (verse) reveals one meaning in the first reading; expands the definition in a new interpretation. The Qur'an's never-ending shine breathes in the soul, heart, and mind. You discover clues that lead to other evidence of new wisdom; understanding trickles like the spring of a holy river, one knowledge, one flow. When you think you have learned all, the Holy Qur'an begins to stream again.

All those who read the Holy Book once, twice or more realize the verses bespeak for every era, place, and time. Millions of non-Muslims study the Holy Book carefully, embracing and practicing the faith in complete devotion. A verse gives you a feeling when you read it; when you genuinely understand the intended message, you feel a soothing storm touring your entire being.

The Holy Qur'an answers all questions, settles all disputes, teaches all the need to know about the Earth, the seven skies, moon, stars, and the sun. It informs us that a mom and dad nourish and parent each living thing. The Holy Qur'an provides clues and directions for new knowledge, such as the

ولا تَحْسَبَنَّ الَّذِينَ قُتِلُواْ فِي سَبِيلِ الله أَمْوَاتًا بَلْ أَحْيَاء عِندَ رَبِّهِمْ يُرْزَقُونَ

Barzegh that separates two oceans or the soul we cannot see. Scientists validate significant discoveries by seeking confirmation from the Holy Qur'an or certified Hadeeths.

Yunus Nef'i gained strength and wisdom from the Holy Book. He learned how to structure his story so the reader can tolerate the emotional pain of some lines and paragraphs. He added merciful parables, short-short stories, and poems, including love episodes close to reality as eyesight. You hear the characters as you read, and your eyes watch the action.

The Holy Qur'an gave the human species twenty-four prophets, pbut. Muhammad pbuh, the twenty-fifth and final messenger, preached Islam with his companions with a passion equal to power to air and water, to the puissance of night and day. Islam changed the world. Slavery died. Misery and poverty disappeared. Mercy returned, and justice and peace reigned.

Islam's ray guided the Earth's heirs, shined on every breathing soul and radiated doubtful hearts. Islam spread to the East and West. Zakat flowed from the deepest valleys to the highest mountains. Birds of Heaven and those of the Earth together celebrated. The moon, the sun, and the stars hurried their rise. Islam uplifted their passion. Creatures of every species above and below receive shared food to maintain a productive life. Out of ignorance and bigotry, the West hid the truth about prophets Adam to Mohammad, pbut for thousands of years. The sun of the truth confirmed Islam was a universal religion for all in the past. It will again touch peace-loving people everywhere.

ALLAH created the oceans, raised the skies without pillars and placed the scale. HE created a Barzegh between oceans, one salty, the other sweet— no storm, hurricane, or atomic power could cause the two to mix. He created Adam from Heaven's clay and Hawa from a rib. "We brought forth from them, men and women" (4:) 1. Qur'an. ALLAH did not say, children. Did HE create eight clones of Adam and, from their ribs, eight moms? Did Adam and Hawa start a family of their own? If so, eight fathers and eight moms had no biological relation, thus making the marriage holy.

That would confirm daughters and sons did not marry to begin a family. Adam and Hawa still began the human species because eight dads and eight

وَلاَ تَحْسَبَنَّ الَّذِينَ قُتِلُواْ فِي سَبِيلِ اللهِ أَمْوَاتًا بَلْ أَحْيَاء عِندَ رَبِّهِمْ يُرْزَقُونَ

moms were off that initial species. But ALLAH knows all the secrets of the birth and death of all creations. We have limited knowledge, which HE allowed us to understand each creation's purpose and need, so all live in harmony and peace regardless of species.

Most humans abused the gift of learning and ignored the Universal Laws set by ALLAH. They ordained gods and partners of HIM when they knew HE is ONE as they know their children. But still spread "untruth," the Universe exploded; pieces settled where they fell in the Solar System. More than that, they deceived the gods and partners they ordained. If Mariam, Isa and Uzair were alive, they would have testified for the CREATOR's ONENESS and called the forgers pathetic liars.

Every time Yunus Nef'i steps outside, his door looks at the sun or watches snowflakes or raindrops falling on the Earth, curses the pathetic liars and forgers, and curses the Mullahs of Farsi-Iran more for spreading hatred and Shi'ism under Islam's name. He asks himself, "Why do most people deny the ONENESS of the CREATOR, add gods and partners who had no control of a street or a neighbourhood but spent their lives on the run and hiding."

An ant, an elephant or a bee refutes all forgeries and assumptions ALLAH has partners; denies other gods; denies the despicable Shi'ite Cult the Mullahs of Faris-Iran fabricated.

Science learned how ants build homes. Architects and building engineers revised building codes according to the rules of the ants. Science also learned why ants split a grain in half and coriander seed in four to prevent blooming. Science proved ants' technological and intellectual advancement but did not understand how an invertebrate the size of one-fifth of a fingertip acquired all this knowledge.

Science failed to understand the process bees use to make honey. Science failed to know how elephants defended Mecca by defying the orders of their masters. The elephants sensed the flying wind of fire racing from the sea and Stellers carrying large rocks and dropping them on the invaders.

وَلَا تَحْسَبَنَّ الَّذِينَ قُتِلُواْ فِي سبِيلِ اللهِ أَمْوَاتًا بَلْ أَحْيَاء عِندَ رَبِّهِمْ يُرْزَقُونَ

CHAPTER FIVE

Jamal Khashoggi's death in Istanbul on October 2, 2018, shocked the entire world. The perpetrators brought a person of Jamal's height and physique and dressed him in Jamal's suit, scarf, fake mustache and short beard, showing the impostor entering and leaving the consulate. The ridiculous film aired on hundreds of news companies sunk the traitors' and infiltrators' plots more rooted in the mud. The infiltrators intended to pin the crime on Turkey by laying a made-believe trail leading to the doorstep of the Saudi Consulate. The imposter entering and leaving the Consulate eluded Jamal Khashoggi's murder happened inside the Consulate. Who sent the pictures from his Apple Watch to his fiance's iPhone is still a very dark clue. The killers drug him with anesthesia and disable his Watch while incinerating or dissolving the body in acid is farfetched. But some pictures had already reached the iPhone. Nearly all countries, including the UN, poets, journalists, writers, authors, and artists condemned the horrendous crime. All believe that Musad and other foreign security agencies planned and carried out the murder of the Saudi journalist.

The Crown Prince denied the accusation he was behind the crime: The infiltrators' coverup and lack of international diplomatic pressure prompted the Saudi Authority to investigate profoundly and thoroughly. The arrest of twenty-three collaborators and other infiltrators who operated not far from the highest offices of the Royal Rulers lifted the suspicions off the Crown Prince. el-Qahtani, the chief aide of Mohammad Ben Selman and alleged architect of the murder, disappeared, not on the run, and the courts did not issue an arrest notice against him. Turkey investigators provided the Saudi Authority with undisputable evidence and continued investigating further— expecting to arrest local infiltrators. Highly ranked security agencies

وَلاَ تَحْسَبَنَّ الَّذِينَ قُتِلُواْ فِي سَبِيلِ اللهِ أَمْوَاتًا بَلْ أَحْيَاء عِندَ رَبِّهِمْ يُرْزَقُونَ

commended the Turkish investigators for revealing the proof at snail's speed, often comparing the murder case to solid rock.

You lose half the evidence if you chip off the pieces too quickly. Investigators gathered nearly all the proof and concluded the perpetrators burned the body in an incinerator oven. That does not mean the murder case is now closed because, thus far, solid and tangible evidence is not sufficient.

Khashoggi's murder left a permanent shameful cloud over freedom of speech and shamed those who continue boasting about Western democracy. Within Khashoggi's murder puzzle, there are several unexamined blocks. Was Khashoggi's exile in Turkey or the United States? Was he a victim of forced recruiting into the CIA? Was his fiance a victim also of the same conspiracy?

His children of his first wife did not believe their father went into exile as he had no reason to do so. He is a journalist of high credibility, respected by his peers, and a profoundly patriotic Saudi; he loved his country and never had any issues with domestic or international laws.

The last block of the puzzle belongs to Trump and Netanyahu, who, behind curtains, applied everything in their power and influence to thwart the relationship between Turkey and Saudi Arabia. Their conspiracy brought effective results but withered after a few years when the Saudis and the Turkish leadership uncovered the stratagem but did not make it public.

The Saudi public prosecutor Saud al-Mojeb came to Istanbul on October 28, 2018. He and his security experts did leave with quite a bit of the proof that remains highly classified evidence, which may never become public information. Turkey released certain speculations to the news media before the Saudi prosecutor's visit. Leading world investigators believe Turkey may have found inconclusive evidence but refused to share it.

Jamal's murder escalated the war in Yemen. That alerted Political scientists from the East and the West to support the theory Trump and Netanyahu's connection with Jamal's murder achieved two goals: Thwarting the relationship between Saudi Arabia and Turkey and escalating the war in Yemen. Farsi-Iran drew the Saudis and the alliance into the war after armed

وَلَا تَحْسَبَنَّ الَّذِينَ قُتِلُواْ فِي سَبِيلِ الله أَمْوَاتًا بَلْ أَحْيَاء عِندَ رَبِّهِمْ يُرْزَقُونَ

the Houthis with ballistic missiles and drones. The Houthis allied with Ali Salah, the former president. Salah broke the alliance with them when he realized Farsi-Iran would eventually occupy his country. Weeks after, the Houthis assassinated him.

The war in Yemen levelled thousands of Yemeni homes, which created a significant epidemic of deadly diseases. Half the devastated country's twenty-three million barely survive for lack of clean water, food, and medicine.

Jamal's peers and readers looked up to him as a non-bias journalist who highlighted the truth in moderate views and offered alternatives to wrongs. He covered the USSR war in Afghanistan and the Farsi-Iran/Iraq war; he covered Saddam's invasion of Kuwait and exposed Iraqi soldiers indiscriminately killed as they retreated under a peace agreement between U.S. and Iraqi commanders. He covered the U.S. invasion of Afghanistan and Iraq.

Yunus Nef'i wrote a score of poems and theses on civilians' blind bombing by U.S. soldiers and the appalling atrocities Israel committed against Palestinians. Western news and Arab media harshly criticized the two journalists.

Yunus and Jamal wrote for Arab News English daily. If Yunus lived in Saudi Arabia, he might have faced Jamal's fate, as his writing reflects injustice and oppression. Jamal thought U.S. soil would be safe. But he did not realize Trump and Netanyahu had already planned their conspiracy. Yunus Nef'i regrets not meeting Jamal face to face in a handshake. He bid farewell to his comrade with a personal message: "Crowned martyr! Enjoy your immortal life. Your family, peers and friends and me, among them, shall always remember you."

وَلَا تَحْسَبَنَّ الَّذِينَ قُتِلُوا فِي سَبِيلِ اللهِ أَمْوَاتًا بَلْ أَحْيَاء عِنْدَ رَبِّهِمْ يُرْزَقُونَ

وَلاَ تَحْسَبَنَّ الَّذِينَ قُتِلُواْ فِي سَبِيلِ اللّهِ أَمْوَاتًا بَلْ أَحْيَاء عِندَ رَبِّهِمْ يُرْزَقُونَ

CHAPTER SIX

Yunus Nef'i realized all that had been discussed and written on civilization clash by most Western scholars resulted in nothing more than assumptions. They referred to their societies as the victim and Islam as the aggressor. At the same time, they did not deny Islam introduced the Shoura Governing System of justice, laws, equality, parliament, institutions, and the first blueprints of a charter of rights ever.

Leaders of the new Crusades, Zionists, and leaders of India, China and Russia continue to spread hatred against Muslims. But the truth has the power of water; no force can hold it down. Adam and Hawa became Muslim on the day they walked. Twenty-four other prophets taught the divine religion principles: Prophet Musa pbuh received the Holy Torah between 1360–1379 BCE. Prophet Isa pbuh received the Holy Bible between 1CE–33 CE. Jibrae'el pbuh descended with the Holy Qur'an and Sunnah Hadiths to Prophet Mohammad pbuh between 611 CE –632 CE. The original copies of the two Holy Books (Torah and Bible, before forged) mirrored perfectly with the Holy Qur'an and vice versa.

Since the mid-sixth century, scholars have found no flaws in Islam or the Holy Qur'an and concluded Islam never posed an issue in the past, not an issue today, nor will it be an issue in the future. Issues plaguing the world are racial violence in the first place, followed by wars, starvation and lust for power.

Psychiatrists and psychologists often conclude, not with any degree of proof, craving for human blood is split-personality syndrome at war with itself. For example, it is impossible for all Crusades' commanders and soldiers, including Pope Urban II, to suffer from split personality syndrome.

وَلاَ تَحْسَبَنَّ الَّذِينَ قُتِلُواْ فِي سَبِيلِ اللّهِ أَمْوَاتًا بَلْ أَحْيَاء عِندَ رَبِّهِمْ يُرْزَقُونَ

The Crusades' nine wars and thirty battles left an estimated 500-mln killed, wounded and maimed, 90% civilians.

In the last two centuries, the Crusades waged wars in the Middle East, Asia and Africa using the Pope's decree against civilians also left tens of millions killed, wounded and maimed.

The West committed an unforgiven crime when it did not include Arabs and Africans in the industrial and technological revolutions. The wheel of fortune that always stopped at the West sooner or later will stop at Africa and the Middle East.

Arabs taught merchandising as trading partners with Asian, European, and African countries. When Islam came, Arabs and Muslims introduced science, mathematics, literature, poetry, philosophy, and arts.

The West created tribal deep-rooted nationalism among Arabs, Africans, Asians, and South and Central Americans. The divide-and-weaken strategy triggered hatred and vengeance. Farsi-Iran fabricated Shi'ism and used Islam and the Holy Qur'an for cover; Zionist clans spread Islamophobia. Right-wing extremists and Christian Evangelists do not want to see any other races on the Earth except white skin.

The West installed dictators to rob natural resources and drive people away from Islam. It held back any self-sufficiency progress but lost the war against Islam. Muslims absorbed their holy religion like water falling on thirsty soil. Non-Muslims embrace Islam daily, while other faiths decline rapidly.

France, England, China, India, Farsi-Iran and Russia started killing Muslims when the old Crusades' slaughtering stopped. Despite wars, dehumanization, and profiling, Muslims have grown faster than the global population. "Of a truth, you are stronger (than they) because of the terror in their hearts, (sent) by ALLAH, they are men devoid of understanding" (59):13 Qur'an.

Farsi-Iran became Islam's worse foe when it allied with the Crusades against the Ottomans, who cherished Arab culture and tradition.

وَلاَ تَحْسَبَنَّ الَّذِينَ قُتِلُواْ فِي سَبِيلِ الله أَمْوَاتًا بَلْ أَحْيَاء عِندَ رَبِّهِمْ يُرْزَقُونَ

It despised Arab nobleness and generousness when it learned these were the reasons for its isolation. Arabs were known for their cunning in trade, which made them wealthy.

Arab poets wrote excellent poetry. An Arab girl represented the absolute honour in a family, a Farsi girl's dream—an Arab knight on a horse to feel honoured, but that never happened.

Farsi-Iran and Iraqi Shi'ites allied with the U.S. during the 2003 invasion. It Opened its borders with Iraq to the invading armies. The U.S. and the traitors circled the Iraqi soldiers with a surprise attack that killed tens of thousands. If Farsi-Iran did not allow the U.S. and the coalition inside Iraq's back door, tens of thousands of the invading soldiers would have died.

Farsi-Iran showed all its venom and hatred. What did Arab dictators do? They paid the total cost of the invasion and continued to funnel cash into the U.S. Treasury. Arab dictators' treason, Farsi-Iran's hatred for Arabs and the West feeding animosity between the two nations left Muslim Sunnis vulnerable to the worse type of profiling and ethnic cleansing.

Yunus Nef'i witnessed conflicts and wars for a quarter of a century, and poetry germinated in his wounds and grief. Political critics tried every conniving trick to derail his efforts; the attack on his pen did not dent his strength; he refused to fall to bigotry and camouflage terrorism. Critics accused him of revealing too much of the truth. He fenced his emotions by recalling the saying, "There is no room for fear when right leads to justice." Bravery buds from the soul. Cowardice sprouts from artificial voice. Yunus Nef'i is old and frail but fit and ready to challenge critics. His domain floats behind a Barzegh; his grit is not a few drops, a little creek or a natural river; it is a sea of thoughts and a sharp pen in a steady hand.

Yunus Nef'i transcribes poems with bruised fingers; each rhymes with his pulse; the page absorbs words like blood consumes oxygen; his heart decides if his journey has reached the end.

As soon as Arab traitors, dictators and invaders perish, he will throw the towel, break the pen and smash the keyboard.

وَلاَ تَحْسَبَنَّ الَّذِينَ قُتِلُواْ فِي سَبِيلِ اللهِ أَمْوَاتًا بَلْ أَحْيَاء عِندَ رَبِّهِمْ يُرْزَقُونَ

Every million trillion spins, the Earth receives new genes, flesh and bone mature, and the soul opens the womb and covers the infant with light visible only to the mother. People of good genes increase, and genetically deformed eventually perish.

If science advances beyond the Seven Skies, it cannot decide the birth rate: Nations with a record majority in the books of history ended up minority; nations with a record minority abused and tortured, moved up to a majority held the truth at heart and worshipped ONE GOD.

Trump venom, Israel's apartheid, Arab traitors, white bigots, Bashar frying his people, Farsi-Iran pouring oil on fire, Putin raining missiles on civilians, science ignoring the birth formula – all cannot and will not decide who survives or rules in the end.

President Donald Trump allied with Zionist Jews, Zionist Arabs and the white-wing extremists, allied with the worse extremists, the Christian Evangelists. Trump unveiled the hidden, untombed, the buried and exposed the leaders of Europe, Asia and the Middle East.

America pre-Donald Trump is not the America of today. He introduced an economic war strategy against his competitors and foes alike. His doctrine will continue beyond his last term in office.

On a scale, American internal racial violence never seen before could surface before or after the next election of 2020. Will the voice of reason come ahead? Americans had seen more falls than rescues since the founding fathers formed the Union. During Obama's two terms, America's superiority declined significantly morally, spiritually and economically. Trump restored the economy but failed on moral and spiritual fronts. Unfortunately, Covid-19 slowed down the world economically and mentally.

Historically Americans play dumb when life goes well. When life becomes shove and push, they bond and rebuild by merely using the existing infrastructure, mend the nation's fractures, and crush bigotry. Could America rise again? America entered a new era when Trump occupied the

وَلاَ تَحْسَبَنَّ الَّذِينَ قُتِلُواْ فِي سَبِيلِ الله أَمْوَاتًا بَلْ أَحْيَاء عِندَ رَبِّهِمْ يُرْزَقُونَ

White House. The world learned more about America's natural face in three years than it knew for three hundred years.

Trump stripped the masks of all previous Administrations. The Upper and Lower Houses conveniently wore masks according to world changes and political climates. The U.S. politically, economically and militarily continues to dominate the world stage. Controlling with unchallenged power always leads to a crash for two main reasons. One: A decline in cautious intellectual planning; two: The crash could also come when the nations it controls and oppresses become loose canons.

The split of Korea created WPK, the most dangerous regime. Russia, on one end, China, on the other, and baby Kim Jong-un short of sufficient power, threaten America. The invasion of Afghanistan and Iraq, the raging flame in the entire Middle East, which had already reached North Africa, gave Farsi-Iran Carte Blanch and left tens of millions without a home; casualties also reached millions of wounded, maimed and killed. If America used the same policy in Japan after the nuclear attack or The Marshall Plan, also known as The Europe Recovery Program, we would have an open, civilized world, disciplined and responsible.

History is a record of events and a clock that rolls back time. Oppressed people lose loved ones to conflicts and wars, tolerate stampeding on rights, starve and suffer. But at some point, anger inflates and deflates the lungs. No suppressed people want to watch the world go forward while they stay at the end of the line.

وَلاَ تَحْسَبَنَّ الَّذِينَ قُتِلُواْ فِي سَبِيلِ اللهِ أَمْوَاتًا بَلْ أَحْيَاء عِندَ رَبِّهِمْ يُرْزَقُونَ

وَلَا تَحْسَبَنَّ الَّذِينَ قُتِلُواْ فِي سَبِيلِ اللّهِ أَمْوَاتًا بَلْ أَحْيَاء عِندَ رَبِّهِمْ يُرْزَقُون

CHAPTER SEVEN

Yunus Nef'i's grief bites off his bones; sorrow ages him; his pen jumps from one holocaust to another. France occupied Algeria from 1834 to 1962 and Syria and Lebanon from 1920 to 1943. The UK scooped Egypt from 1882–1922 and Palestine from 1920 –1948. World War I from 1914 to 1918 and War II from 1939 to 1945 destroyed most of Europe. The UK offered Palestine to Zionist terrorists. Terrorists accepted the ransom and stopped bombing cities in Europe. The UK supplied Arabs helping the Palestinians with old rifles, supplied the Zionist cannons and tanks, and created a battalion under Laurence of Arabia. The brigade provided intelligence to Zionists.

Palestine fell in 1948. Documents circulated among media gurus, journalists and news companies revealed a savage ethnic cleansing between 1948–1950 in the four-hundred villages and towns. West Bank and East el-Quds remained under Jordon; Egypt controlled Gaza. The UN passed a resolution on May 11, 1949, recognizing Israel as a state.

The UK also used the barter trade against Arab el-Awaz in 1925 and Abu Musa, Greater Tunb, and Lesser Tunb Islands of the UAE in 1972 for interest in Farsi-Iran's oil fields. The U.K. went beyond occupation and murder. It traded land and resources it did not own, ruined the people's social fabric, and robbed every place it occupied.

Israel occupied Sinai, Gaza, the West Bank, east el-Quds, the Golan Heights and the Jordan Valley during the 1967 war. Israel expelled thousands of Palestinians to nearby countries, killed half of those who stayed, and classified survivors as third-class citizens. Israel brought Zionists from everywhere, the majority non-Jews. It built tens of thousands of settlements

وَلاَ تَحْسَبَنَّ الَّذِينَ قُتِلُواْ فِي سَبِيلِ اللّهِ أَمْوَاتًا بَلْ أَحْيَاء عِندَ رَبِّهِمْ يُرْزَقُونَ

on stolen land. It issued laws that forced Palestinian families to destroy their homes or pay the authorities a massive fine for demolition.

Egypt recovered Sinai in the 1973 war under President Sadat. The Israeli army retreated with shattered ego and pride. Sadat's victory shuddered the dignity of America and Europe. The CIA, Mubarak, and Mossad plotted to assassinate Sadat after the U.S. brokered peace between Israel, Egypt, Syria and Jordon. Egyptian courts framed the Muslim Brotherhood for the murder and prosecuted one of its members. CIA, Mossad and Mubarak walked free; Mubarak became president; Hafez el-Assad gave the Golen Heights to Israel as a token of friendship; Jordon stuck to the peace accord.

Jewish leftists and Torah Jews represent 60% of Israel. They rejected David Ben Gurion's expansionist dream and all the other prime ministers, except for Isaac Robin, who served two terms: 1974–1977, and 1992–1995, the year Zionist Jews assassinated him. Anwar Sadat and Isaac Robin almost ended decades of conflicts and wars. The world missed one chance in a million after the assassination of two peace champions. That chance may never come with the Zionist Lobby controlling all joints of America, Europe, and Arab dictators stabbing Palestinians in the back. Palestinian Arabs, Torah Jews, and other ethnicities lived in the region from the river to the sea. All forebears came from Yemen, the original birthplace of the human species.

As the West learned about Arab wealth, they plotted against the region. The French seized most natural resources in North Africa. The resistance fought the French occupation, and the proxy leaders for nearly a hundred and thirty years gave one million martyrs. Tens of thousands perished through seven nuclear attacks—the French claimed were experiments only.

The Arab Peninsula sat on the world's largest oil and gas fields. Arabs did not know the value of that wealth. The UK knew after the French tutored them. At their cost, the UK offered to drill the wells, extract and refine the oil and gas, and take care of selling and shipping.

King Abdulaziz Al Saud favoured U.S. oil companies because of his close ties with President Franklin Roosevelt. The U.S. became the tenant rent-free but paid the landlord a percentage, keeping most of the net profit by

وَلاَ تَحْسَبَنَّ الَّذِينَ قُتِلُواْ فِي سَبِيلِ الله أَمْوَاتًا بَلْ أَحْيَاء عِندَ رَبِّهِمْ يُرْزَقُونَ

inflating costs. King Faisal, who said enough, imposed an oil embargo on America and Europe during the 1973 war. In 1988 the Kingdom nationalized all-natural resource fields, including precious metal mines.

Palestine was not the only thing the Zionists went after. In 1889, Zionism adopted the Urban hateful ideology, instigated World War I and II, controlled and supported the side with the upper hand, and watched the other's destruction. Depression left millions jobless; famine soared; civilian casualties surpassed one hundred million and destroyed half of Europe. American, British, French, and Russian soldiers raped two million women, most of whom were German.

Zionists bought land and properties for a fraction of the actual value and built a new banking system that tied all countries in a bind, making all payments and transfers clear through one channel they controlled. The U.S. engaged Europe in a forced marriage. Other countries like China and Japan took the road of economic development.

The Zionists established sexual orgies, gambling, alcohol, drugs, great food and erotic entertainment. The wealthy paid substantial membership fees. Influential military personnel, chief executive officers, and heads of state got free admission as they pulled strings favouring Israel. Clients came from the upper class of renowned figures, wealthy dictators from various public and private sectors, the media, writers, actors, poets, and university deans. Mossad blackmailed every patron with an offence such as bribery, fraud, prostitution, and in some cases, murder to prevent defection. The Zionist Chiefs recruited military sales executives from highly advanced countries, paid hefty bribes, and connected local spies with the Mossad. Israel became a nuclear power with the latest air, naval, and ground forces.

Arab traitors and military generals propelled sectarian conflict and involved parties into sporadic civil war precisely to Israel's wishes. Zionists established organizations to penetrate Western social and human rights groups that supported the aspiration of Palestinians. Zionists control the U.S. and European institutions, the UN, and NATO. Zionists suppress activists, journalists, poets, scholars, writers, and artists for speaking or writing against apartheid, suppress reports on blind killing, starvation,

وَلاَ تَحْسَبَنَّ الَّذِينَ قُتِلُواْ فِي سَبِيلِ اللهِ أَمْوَاتًا بَلْ أَحْيَاء عِندَ رَبِّهِمْ يُرْزَقُونَ

shutting borders, confiscating properties, and withholding taxes and donations. On a leash, U.S. and European leaders served Israel on hands and knees. Zionism split the Middle East into two: One side struggles to survive; it controls the other.

Israel lost Hosni Mubarak to the Arab Spring sweep on January 26, 2011, but gained Abdul Fattah Assisi. Asissi toppled President Mohammad Mursi on July 3, 2013, placed him in solitary prison, tortured and denied him essential medication, proper food and clean water. The prison's doctor injected Mursi with a poisonous serum on the way to the courtroom. The judge ordered the state's lawyers to call an ambulance after forty minutes; the judge contributed to the murder on June 17, 2019.

Assisi banned a public funeral, allowing only a few family members to attend the burial. Egyptian Security posted guards around the grave 24/7. No objection came out from any U.S., European or Arab officials about the mysterious assassination of President Mursi. On the 23rd and 24th of May 2012, Mursi won the presidency in two rounds through a ballot system monitored by a dozen countries.

Assisi's seven-year rule brought Egypt to its knees. Inflation soared by 200%; 70% of corporations moved elsewhere; the national debt rose by twenty folds; the jobless ratio jumped over fifty percent. Fifty million Egyptians survive on a half meal a day; thirty-nine million eat half every second day. Jewish Zionists rule Egypt and poison it socially, economically, and morally. Local security forces arrest people on fabricated terrorism charges. Correctional officers torture prisoners daily. Assisi will not stop killing Sinai people until his soldiers kill the last person and destroy the endmost home. All oppositions held in prisons will die by hanging. Hanging in Egypt under Assisi has surpassed the global number ten folds. The U.N. and its branch on human rights sporadically make a statement after Western leaders' objection, which usually disappears after the news conference.

Zionist prime ministers and U.S. and Europe leaders secretly debated relocating all Palestinians to Sinai. Trump activated the plan and agreed to invest in infrastructure projects at the Gulf States' expense. Trump took the first step. He declared el-Quds the new capital of Israel and moved the U.S.

وَلاَ تَحْسَبَنَّ الَّذِينَ قُتِلُواْ فِي سَبِيلِ اللهِ أَمْوَاتًا بَلْ أَحْيَاء عِندَ رَبِّهِمْ يُرْزَقُونَ

Embassy from Tel Aviv. Trump undressed the secret deal of the century when he massed naval fleets and frigates in waterways and posted military forces on the ground. Present governments knew about the Zionists' plan.

Trump rules the rulers of Egypt and blackmails the Gulf States. Assisi's army is close to clearing Sinai of people. Israel already has prepared a plan to annex the West Bank, Gaza, and east el-Quds and expel Palestinians, including the ones inside the Green Line, to a non-militarized zone in Northern Sinai. Saudi Arabia, the UAE and tiny Bahrain will likely pay a lump sum (in billions) to Jordan, Syria, Iraq, and Lebanon to grant citizenship to Palestinians living on their soil. Trump and European leaders also agreed to receive tens of thousands of displaced families.

Trump's insane treason virus in the Middle East could repeat America's dark history when the sheriff's law ruled. That jungle system killed tens of millions of Natives and Blacks. The Christian Church's Clergies used ethnic cleansing that consisted of deadly bacteria implanted in food, water, and blankets. They forced alcohol on Natives whose blood type reacted to the beverage as a lethal injunction would. Human rights activists then did not exist but surfaced after the Union's rules replaced the sheriff's law.

Could Natives and Blacks have taken up arms? Resisting would not have survived the terror of Christian clergies and the new Union's forces. Did the founders of America learn a lesson from such a horrifying past? The influx of immigrants shifted the attention from the killing to the building. In less than a century, America became the most attractive country in the world. It earned the motto "The land of the Free and the Brave."

The Zionists dragged America into World War I and II. On the 7th of December 1941, Japan bombed Pearl Harbour; on August 6, 1946, a U.S. naval base retaliated not with "an eye for an eye." It nuked Hiroshima, killed 80,000 civilians, and levelled nearly thirty thousand buildings; the effects of the fallout reaped another 60,000 lives, and tens of thousands suffered through prolonged death. On August 9, 1946, it nuked Nagasaki killing 35,000, 20,000 died of fallout result, and thousands died of protracted death, destroying many buildings and homes.

وَلاَ تَحْسَبَنَّ الَّذِينَ قُتِلُواْ فِي سَبِيلِ اللّهِ أَمْوَاتًا بَلْ أَحْيَاء عِندَ رَبِّهِمْ يُرْزَقُونَ

The U.S. and the USSR tricked each other into invading other countries; each supported one side of the conflict. Thousands of U.S. and USSR soldiers sacrificed their lives for a pitiful competition, "who gets to invade first." Survivors of the impaired psychologically became suicide candidates; the wheelchair victims and stable ones spoke out against wars. U.S. military laws provided a pension for the survivors' families and the injured. The USSR neglected war survivors and did little for the wounded.

The Korean War with the U.S. directly split South and North, leaving nearly three million dead and several million wounded. 40,000 Americans died in action, and 100,000 were injured. The U.S. waged another war against Communist Viet Cong: mid-range civilian casualties stood at over two million killed and more than a million wounded between 1955–1975. Other estimates show casualties of resistant fighters and U.S. soldiers at 200,000 dead and twice that number injured. Atrocities and the destruction of villages, towns, and cities did not shake the world. The U.S. bombarded Vietnam by air, ground, and sea.

Political gurus exposed the use of Mustard Gas to force Uncle Sam to stop the war. The efforts thawed the frozen emotions of a few top generals. Jane Fonda, an American celebrity, opposed the war and voiced her anger at every campus. Millions of students joined her peace drive. She shook the conscience of Americans. Nixon recalled many troops; President Ford officially ended the war. The U.S. called for a ceasefire. Seventeen years of ongoing attacks and bombings did not break the Vietnamese fighters' volition or determination armed with mediocre weapons against a superpower.

France mediated the peace for months; exerted tremendous pressure on the Vietnamese commandoes, who refused to stop fighting unless the U.S. accepted defeat. The French witnessed the accord and released a copy as the secrecy protection lapsed.

The U.S. fought thirteen wars, including World War I and II, at 18.2 trillion dollars. The 2008/2009 financial crash wiped out 19.2 trillion; human casualties stood at over fifteen million killed and maimed. How did the U.S.

وَلَا تَحْسَبَنَّ الَّذِينَ قُتِلُواْ فِي سَبِيلِ اللهِ أَمْوَاتًا بَلْ أَحْيَاء عِندَ رَبِّهِمْ يُرْزَقُونَ

stay afloat? 90% of the 19.2 trillion belonged to Arab investors. Despite that investment loss, wealthy Arabs continued to funnel cash into U.S. banks.

Venezuela, the recent victim of a coup not far from its doors, expects a U.S. air attack first and a vicious civil war to follow. Yunus Nef'i already picked the title "U.S. versus Russia." Watch for a Latino Spring in Central and South America, where over half a billion people do not have Che Guevara or Fidel Castro to lead and control. Putin believes he is now the lion (forever grateful to Obama); he believes Biden is a rooster with no feathers. If the rooster with no feathers skins the lion, America will become a sacred chicken farm. Putin will move to Siberia, fish and drink Vodka.

Biden, Vladimir Putin, Narendra Modi, and Xi Jinping hold sufficient power to destroy the entire world in a nuclear catastrophe. Or each leader plunges into an internal conflict - - people killing each other as European Christian savages did during the war of acquisition in the 16, 17, and early 18th centuries.

The USSR and China caused the death of nearly a hundred million during internal unrest. The USSR killed millions of Afghanis and destroyed 75% of the country. Arab and Afghani Mujahedeen won in the end and caused the fragmentation of the USSR. Putin's catastrophic war in Syria forced five million helpless people into Iraq, Turkey, Jordon, and Lebanon, not including the hundreds of thousands butchered.

The Indian regime starves the people but spends billions on the war against the two provinces, Kashmir and Jammu. Since 1989 Indian soldiers committed mass killings, enforced torture, repression, disappearance, rape, and freedom suppression. Two hundred thousand civilians have died.

The Indian Government recently stepped on Kashmir and Jammu's self-rule, which the U.N. approved in 1948. India wants to scoop the two provinces using terrorism pretence for a cause. In the nineteenth century, India annexed 48% of Kashmir, Pakistan got 35%, and China 17%. Three wars between India and Pakistan left one million dead. Scooping Kashmir and Jammu could trigger a war and lead to a nuclear holocaust, destroying both nations.

ولاَ تَحْسَبَنَّ الَّذِينَ قُتِلُواْ فِي سبِيلِ اللهِ أَمْواتًا بَلْ أَحْياءَ عِندَ رَبِّهِمْ يُرْزَزُقُونَ

The Indo-Israel Friendship Association holds a frequent public discussion on Zionism and Hindutva. The two ideologies, spirited in fascism and Nazism, occupied headlines right after the Indian government announced its intention to annex Kashmir and Jammu. Theodor Herzi and V.D. Savarkar's posters and famous quotes fill the walls of convocation halls.

China holds three million Uighurs in prison camps only because they are Muslims. It forces them to eat pork, drink liquor, cannot pray, or go to mosques. Burma's soldiers committed a holocaust against Herenga Muslims in the Province of Arakan. Families died under pyramids of flames. Soldiers torched homes and properties to ashes and forced a million into neighbouring countries.

El-Ahwaz (an Arab land) of eleven million, thirty-two times the size of Lebanon, held 80% of the oil and gas fields before being traded by the UK. Three major rivers, Karoon, Jarrahi, and Karkheh, provided overwhelming agricultural and fishing revenues to Ahwazes. Ayatollah Khomeini redirected the rivers to other territories, scooped the oil and gas fields and declared them government properties. He isolated El-Ahwaz from the outside world to mask the daily hanging and repression.

El-Ahwaz's population today amounts to three million—Arab indignant without clean water. Electricity and food became scarce. Farsi-Iran confiscated most of the land and homes. Every place the UK occupied left disintegrated on all levels and planted seeds of sectarian wars.

Farsi-Iran invented apartheid and applied it throughout history; the Ahwazes got worse. White rulers of South Africa enrolled thousands of white terrorists and military officers in Mullahs' classrooms. The Zionists cloned the curriculum and established a branch in Israel. Farsi-Iran sent psychopath deans to Iraq, Syria, Yemen, and Lebanon, who founded chapters that recruited tens of thousands of terrorists.

Arabia sits on fire; Farsi-Iran and Israel export the flame; Shi'ite militias kill Sunnis, destroy mosques and build Hussieniates. Israel demolishes Palestinian homes and kills and imprisons the young and the old. Two breeds are not of human genes; one uses Islam for cover, and the other uses Judaism.

وَلَا تَحْسَبَنَّ الَّذِينَ قُتِلُواْ فِي سَبِيلِ اللهِ أَمْوَاتًا بَلْ أَحْيَاء عِندَ رَبِّهِمْ يُرْزَقُونَ

The world flipped, and so did the conscience of most leaders. 10% control 90% of the food, water, and wealth. The World Bank controls the controllers. White supremacists of the U.S. and Europe run for public office in the various ridings and win seats.

The murder of fifty Muslims in two mosques in Christchurch, New Zealand, signalled that all the talk about Western values, freedom of speech and religious rights never applied to Muslims or other minorities.

The Arab world sits on a mobile volcano as mighty as the recent fire in the Amazon Forest. The portable volcano moves as directed by blood-thirsty white supremacist leaders and bigots like Trump, Netanyahu, Macron and Putin, including dictators like Narendra Modi, Xi Jinping, Ali Khameini, Bashar and Assisi. The volcano also moves as directed by honchos of terrorist groups like Hassan Nasrallah, Abdul-Malik Badreddin al-Houthi and Abdullah Ocalan.

Ninety percent of Arabs and Iranians struggle to meet basic needs; millions live below poverty—starvation and disease cause the death of 7.9 citizens per 1000. Jobless fluctuates between 30% and 50%. Dictators block scientists and educators who want to help people move ahead and build a future. They muzzle the voice, the pen, and the brush. If the governments allocate 10% of the wealth toward education and economic development, 90% of poverty and diaspora will disappear.

The region's masses must bank on the Arab Spring and focus on Turkey's progress; they might find an Erdogan among them. Thus far, the Arab Spring has helped eliminate brutal dictators like Mubarak, Khadafi, Ben Ali, Ali Salah, Boutefliak and el-Bashir. Bashar hangs on a straw; an imminent rope waits for Khamenei, Netanyahu, Assisi, Aoun, Nesrallah and Beri, Putin, Narendra Modi, and Xi Jinping.

Arabs, Iranians, and other Muslims who left their native land and settled in other countries contributed commendably to all essential fronts. Tens of millions live in Europe, the Americas, Africa, and Asia. Many hold degrees in various fields; teach in university faculties, lead science, medicine, and engineering; own viable businesses of essential needs and services.

وَلاَ تَحْسَبَنَّ الَّذِينَ قُتِلُواْ فِي سَبِيلِ اللهِ أَمْوَاتًا بَلْ أَحْيَاء عِندَ رَبِّهِمْ يُرْزَقُونَ

They generate hundreds of billions of dollars for their new countries. Despite the excellent contribution, Western leaders, including Mullahs, Zionists, and white bigots, unjustly accuse Arabs and Muslims of 99% of world murder, terrorism, theft, narcotics and women's abuse. The conspiracy does not gear toward conviction, as 99% of the allegations hold no legal worth but are false and untrue.

To keep Islamophobia in the news, bigots will continue to rape uprightness as long the Zionist Lobby controls all joints of America and Europe and as long dictators of Farsi-Iran and infiltrators move freely in Arab countries. Abuse of uprightness will continue as long the modern-day Crusades support Israel's ethnic cleansing of Palestinians but overlook France's crimes against humanity in Algeria, other parts of the Middle East and Africa. Abuse of uprightness will continue as long as modern-day Crusades overlook the U.S. and UK's holocausts against Asia and most of the Middle East.

The New Crusades accuse the Ottomans of unproven atrocities against Armenians. Erdogan offered to open the files of six hundred and fifty years. The files contain evidence the Crusades enlisted local traitors, Armenians, and other minorities as mercenary terrorists. Traitors carried out the atrocities. Turks suffered an enormous casualty; Armenians and other minorities suffered the least.

Erdogan asked Europe and the U.S. leaders to bring forward the hard evidence they continue to claim to have. Not one leader stood before the camera or responded to his call.

وَلاَ تَحْسَبَنَّ الَّذِينَ قُتِلُواْ فِي سَبِيلِ اللهِ أَمْوَاتًا بَلْ أَحْيَاء عِندَ رَبِّهِمْ يُرْزَقُونَ

CHAPTER EIGHT

Britain, France, and Israel attacked Egypt in 1956 for control of the Suez Canal. The U.S. stopped the aggression because of the industrial revolution's success, and the need for natural resources increased—the Middle East oil and gas in the fifties were worth trillions of dollars.

The West's industrial revolution accelerated forward at an impressive speed; the Arabs moved backward. The U.S. held on the region as if a magnet's sky fell on it, installed thousands of agents, and expanded its diplomatic presence in Saudi Arabia; it posted land, air, and sea forces in the region. Arab oil wealth is what built America and Europe we know today.

The Zionist Lobby, too, envisioned the region's wealth, moved from Europe to the U.S., and invested heavily in various industries in New York, Chicago, and Detroit. It used the exact blueprint of influence that controlled all the joints of Europe. The Lobby feared the U.S. love affair with Gulf States leaders and the overwhelming Muslim majority of the Middle East. It pushed Islamophobia in the U.S. and throughout Europe; financed caricature artists, newsmakers and filmmakers who produced commercial work profiling Arabs and Muslims as the bad guys. By the end of the twentieth century, movie profiling died down after the industry lost tens of millions of viewers.

How did the Zionists incite a racial war for centuries to this day? America's governing branches, Arab dictators and European leaders became devout proxies of Israel. The CIA played the Robinhood in Arabia, robbed the rich and the poor, recruited and trained informers, and provided graduates with green cards, bank accounts and protection. Since Palestine's occupation, Israel has never stopped developing schemes to deplete the region's assets

ولاَ تَحْسَبَنَّ الَّذِينَ قُتِلُواْ فِي سَبِيلِ اللَّهِ أَمْوَاتًا بَلْ أَحْيَاء عِند رَبِّهِمْ يُرْزَقُونَ

and to incite hatred among the locals. The theft increased dramatically with Trump's presidency.

The U.S. and the Zionist Organization raised dictators from the cradle. They removed Farsi-Iran's Prime Minister Mohammad Mosaddegh in a conspiracy known as the 28 Morad coup d'etat 1953 and installed Mohammad Reza Pahlavi, the Shah. One short phrase of the Shah, "Israel's next war is mine," cost him the throne in 1979. Khomeini became the ruler and spiritual leader through a staged revolution by the U.S. and France. Another swift coup of 1979 removed Ahmed Hassan al-Bakr, President of Iraq and replaced him with Saddam. Saddam used threats against Israel to promote his nationalism. The U.S. showed no regard to the matter but incited the 22 September 1980 war between Sadam and Khomeini, which lasted eight years, left three million dead and injured hundreds of thousands.

Loverboy Clinton gave the world a break; the credit rightfully goes to Monica Lewinsky, who appeased the sexual craving of the pervert President. Under George Bush Sr. and in 1990, the U.S. pumped Saddam in a heroic talk. Saddam ate the bate and invaded Kuwait. The U.S. and its Allies liberated Kuwait quickly, but the ban on all trade and financial resources stayed in force against the Iraqi people. The U.S. tightened the regulation to the maximum on foodstuff imports. Over one million Iraqi children died of starvation. The U.S. and coalition sent thousands of secret agents and recruited thousands of informers, pooled from private and public sectors.

Bush Jr. and Blair invaded Iraq in 2003 under the pretext Sadam hoarded weapons of mass destruction. Army of Shi'ite traitors and Gulf dictators backed the invasion, which wiped out three-quarters of Iraq, murdered and injured two million. The central bank, the oil fields and the galleries fell into the U.S. military, warlords and Shi'ite traitors. No weapons of mass destruction showed up. The invasion reduced Iraq to the stone age. The Gulf States paid for the Farsi-Iran/Iraq war's cost of 1980, Kuwait's liberation in 1991, including Afghanistan's invasion costs of 2001 and Iraq in 2003.

Obama's madness far exceeded that of Bush Jr. and Blair. Did a magic spell infect his eyes and ears that dihydrated his brain? Cowardice is the source

ولا تَحْسَبَنَّ الَّذِينَ قُتِلُواْ فِي سَبِيلِ اللَّهِ أَمْوَاتًا بَلْ أَحْيَاء عِند رَبِّهِمْ يُرْزَقُونَ

of his brain damage. On December 5, 2011, the Iranian Airforce shot down Rq-170, a Sentinel drone of Stealth technology. Iran threatened to pass Stealth to the Russians. Obama bowed to the pressure, signed the nuclear deal, lifted all sanctions, freed frozen assets, and provided access to the global financial system and international banks. Iran fooled five other partners of the nuclear deal: It ran two atomic programs. One adhered to the nuclear agreement, the other developed long-range ballistic missiles, and maybe, not far from a nuclear bomb. Russia got the Stealth technology and helped Iran to clone Rq-170, naming it Shahid-171. The Israelis intercepted the clone on February 12, 2018, and confirmed a spit-image copy.

President Trump moved into the White House on January 20, 2017. On May 8, 2018, he withdrew from the Iran deal. Farsi-Iran's ethnic cleansing against Sunnis caused a flood of refugees bigger than War I and II. Russia, China, Germany, the UK, and France opposed the agreement because Faris-Iran's war against Sunnis was also their war.

But Trump changed all the rules, unveiled the veiled and dug up the buried, dropped all U.S. support for Shi'ites and encouraged Israel to ally with Arab states. Trump does not want America to lose a massive mine of wealth and see Russia, China and Europe fill their pockets and Farsi-Iran dominate the region.

Trump recognizes Europe does not have the military power or desire to police the troubled spots. Russia is weak economically and cannot maintain a massive military force or sustain significant conflicts. China is busy torturing and executing Uighur Muslims daily. Gandhi bailed India from sectarian and racial wars; he believed in dying for but not for totalitarianism, and bigots claimed democracy. Unfortunately, Modi Narendra, the new dictator, took India back before Gandhi.

The cost of war and military presence in sixty countries could have built ten Americas. President Trump opted for economic wars, yielding an actual return and saving lives and money.

America before Obama enjoyed superiority on all fronts. Obama shook that image; Trump killed that perception and introduced "protection services, mobster's style." Arab dictators offered Trump billions to remove Farsi-

وَلَا تَحْسَبَنَّ الَّذِينَ قُتِلُواْ فِي سَبِيلِ اللهِ أَمْوَاتًا بَلْ أَحْيَاء عِندَ رَبِّهِمْ يُرْزَقُونَ

Iran from Arab land. He grabbed the offer and cashed it, gave Netanyahu el-Quds for Israel's capital and half the West Bank to settlers. Arab leaders got nothing. But Trump did box Farsi-Iran on its knees. Once he secures his next instalment from his clients, he will tie the rope around the Mullahs' necks and ask them to leave or face hanging.

Trump replaced the historical animosity between Israel and Arab leaders with a warm relationship, with Arabs as the lucky brides and Israel as the single groom. The current marriage will not last with one stud and many prostitutes, and America's foreign policy favours Israel 110%.

But the alliance still threatens Farsi-Iran to a deep state of hysteria. Arab and Israeli forces represent the first row of attack; U.S. land, sea, and air forces shadow the entire region from four positions. Revolutionary Guards can no longer reach their regional proxies and cannot challenge the enemy face-to-face. Farsi-Iran never fought well in any of its wars or battles when it faced the enemy face-to-face. In Iraq, its militias hit vague targets and ran. Israel bombs its barricades in Syria routinely. The best response is, "Will retaliate at the right time from the right place." That right time never came; Israeli bombers continued to strike their bases in Syria and Iraq, including Yemen. The Musad assassinate scientists and critical political and military personnel.

The Arab Spring swept Algeria and Sudan with eyes on Egypt and the Gulf States. Yunus Nef'i envisions an imminent end to Arab traitors, infiltrators, and the Farsi-Iran regime; sees the U.S. drifting into the unknown.

Most people realized that criminals disguised in seminarian fronts market democracy. After cloning capitalism, the USSR shrunk freedom, including human rights, and perished. Capitalism started to crack slowly at all seams.

The World Bank poses the next threat. Trump inadvertently exposed the threatening plan when he declared an economic war against China, Europe and other countries. Did Trump and the Zionist Lobby author the new threat? They did, indeed. The World Bank sits in the controlling seat of governing institutions. Parliaments are American, Israeli and European Zionist leaders. Russia, China, India, and Farsi-Iran target Islam and are prepared to use nuclear weapons if necessary. The World Bank wants to see

وَلاَ تَحْسَبَنَّ الَّذِينَ قُتِلُواْ فِي سَبِيلِ الله أَمْوَاتًا بَلْ أَحْيَاء عِندَ رَبِّهِمْ يُرْزَقُونَ

a world without Islam but strengthen the positions of Arab traitors. It adopted the blueprint of Pope Urban II's decree of ethnic cleansing. The nine Crusades wars and thirty battles did not go as expected. The blind bombing killed Christians twenty times more than Muslims.

Will Christians be the prominent victims again? The faith's population declined during the Crusades wars and continued to shrink. Christians follow their religion symbolically, and nothing more, not for lack of devotion: Safer to say they seek the truth clergies have failed to provide. Urban's decree was never a tenant of Christianity. The one-time most popular faith today hangs on a spindle and dwindles weekly.

Less fortunate nations no longer accept the Bible for food and water. Missionaries and colonizers stole resources and occupied land. Ottawa, of one million, is an example: On a given Friday, forty thousand Muslims jam mosques of one hundred thirty thousand, and many do not attend prayers. A few thousand Christians of a population of 800,000 attend Sunday's sermon in all city churches combined. Despite the severe drop, Christians face no Christianophobia, ongoing suppression, or terrorism.

وَلاَ تَحْسَبَنَّ الَّذِينَ قُتِلُواْ فِي سَبِيلِ اللّهِ أَمْوَاتًا بَلْ أَحْيَاء عِندَ رَبِّهِمْ يُرْزَقُونَ

وَلاَ تَحْسَبَنَّ الَّذِينَ قُتِلُواْ فِي سَبِيلِ اللهِ أَمْوَاتًا بَلْ أَحْيَاء عِندَ رَبِّهِمْ يُرْزَقُونَ

CHAPTER NINE

Yunus Nef'i's pen has crossed the boundaries between the first human murder and the last of the current war. He grew a bionic sense of a hamster's ear and the heart of a prophet. But that did not save him from feeling lost in a forest denser than the Amazon.

Yunus Nef'i brings a clear conscience in pen, a progeny of a Yemeni tribe six thousand years before Prophet Isa pbuh, born in a village where tropes grow in fields of very high elevation. He lived nearly three-quarters of a century in Canada. He humours Canadian friends with a piece of history: His great-grandfather landed in Montreal in the eighteenth century and lived one hundred and twenty years. Canada was not much older than him when he died.

Canadian mosaic culture contributed to Yunus Nef'i's passion for writing. He wrote poems free from traditional guides and rules. The various cultures and cafés inspired themes and roused education from experiments and practice during a long literary journey. His poetry survived in an expandable womb that moves with time; words mate with cultures and speak many tongues. The boy wished for "snow;" ALLAH fulfilled his dream; Canada proudly added the youngster to her family.

Born to write lit the first candle. Sonnets grew behind high gates; poems hung on walls of cells; thoughts fell like rain on a life of many paths. Poetry lived in a dark world and collected crime scene accounts; crime transcripts depleted tears and soothed broken hearts; prophecy on ice touched the reader's eye, pleased the spirit and consoled the soul. Love moments did not rust with age; romance with death opened a sea of thoughts. The paradise ALLAH downsized to a womb confirmed the holiness of mothers; snowflakes descended; martyrs ascended.

وَلاَ تَحْسَبَنَّ الَّذِينَ قُتِلُواْ فِي سَبِيلِ اللهِ أَمْوَاتًا بَلْ أَحْيَاء عِنْد رَبِّهِمْ يُرْزَقُونَ

Yunus refined and over-refined his metaphors, so his poetry earned martyrdom.

The language, the brain, and all five senses feed Yunus' pen. Critics consider his style an orphan that carries tropes of alien literature. They did not know orphans have a special place in ALLAH's Mercy.

Critics consider Yunus Nef'i a rebel because he would not accept Canada's literature as a by-product of Shakespearian poetry and Guy de Maupassant's short story. Literature existed for centuries before the two literary giants. Writing is the purest confession of the human mind, blueprints that naturally form accordingly. If justice ever conquers, not two styles will look alike.

The internet brings information to the surface with a stroke of a key. Template literature has become a commodity on demand for hasty authors. Template trash affects writing as acid rain poisons nature. Template trash controls most communication means throughout the world. The few authors and poets left to defend the real literature may never beat scam artists and forgers.

Where literary martyrs fall, imposters live. To understand a culture, follow the literature of the people and befriend nature. What you cannot express in writing, you find answers in nature's landscapes and skies. The story of languages is almost identical to human creation. The words perform the role of genes. If we examine the social genetic system, we see a near-likeness of the evolving process.

Writing is a gift that naturally develops from within. It finds its path free of cloning, pure as the soul of a martyr. Trees grow from a bud and breastfeed sap to limbs. Good literature builds unique emotions and also brings countless images before starving readers. Eyes mix millions of colours and shades far ahead of the power of NikonD4 and lenses Nikon24. There is no limit to the human imagination if the eyes, the mind, the soul, and the heart keep creating original thoughts.

Writing that does not breathe has no soul. Those who play ripples with literature should walk to a riverbank and throw the rocks they believe float.

وَلاَ تَحْسَبَنَّ الَّذِينَ قُتِلُواْ فِي سَبِيلِ اللّهِ أَمْوَاتًا بَلْ أَحْيَاء عِندَ رَبِّهِمْ يُرْزَقُونَ

Love cannot survive without poetry; trees conceive limbs and deliver leaves, bees and mates, flowers and roses prove no science can replicate their honey. The sun rises and sets; the moon brings out the stars; every creation carries writing genes.

Yunus Nef'i, the philosopher, scholar, poet, journalist, and author, never cared for these labels. He dedicated his entire literary life to the have-not, the oppressed, and those who lost loved ones and homes to vicious invaders and dictators. He fought for justice and truth; pen, ink and paper were his weapons; his five senses guided his way and helped him see black and white.

He showed no respect for liars, forgers, and idol lovers and despised those who profess democracy based on gains by invading other countries to steal resources and assets. How many conspicuous mindless humans and how many leaders do we have on our planet of these groups? Recap the casualty, destruction, misery, and grief, pick a number, and add nine zeros for the least estimate.

ولاَ تَحْسَبَنَّ الَّذِينَ قُتِلُواْ فِي سَبِيلِ اللهِ أَمْواتًا بَلْ أَحْياء عِندَ رَبِّهمْ يُرْزَقُون

وَلاَ تَحْسَبَنَّ الَّذِينَ قُتِلُواْ فِي سَبِيلِ اللهِ أَمْوَاتًا بَلْ أَحْيَاء عِندَ رَبِّهِمْ يُرْزَقُونَ

CHAPTER TEN

The ten-year-old Yunus Nef'i realized his village (el-Hutaib) stands on an elevation of more than ten thousand feet above sea level and two thousand feet above the clouds. His yearning for snow burned his soul in winter. Three years later, his passion opened the buds of his creative life when he and his family arrived at the Port of Montreal on November 18, 1944.

One drive to the Gatineau Hills with a friend spanned his vision over cotton fields. Thoughts of mirrors reflected on fluffy clouds that slept on each roof. Icicles dripped from water gutters like ropes of crystal. Soul joined his heart; his mind sat in his palm, Arabic poetry roamed over his head and showered him in baby metaphors. Snowflakes gracefully fell on the hills; the Arabic alphabet united in a triplet of kin and matching genes.

Recollections of el-Hutaib still dodge in his mind like the scent of a rose that surfs the space looking for a bee. He would be standing under the beam of the front door, reading a poem wishing for a miracle to happen so the village receives her share of rain and snow. He wanted the friends he left behind to feel the joy of touching and playing in the snow. Somehow, his instinct tells him one day, that miracle will happen.

The recollections drift from the village to the sea journey: Metaphors poured from a blue sky, mountain waves rocked the old ship, swirled the boy, and wrestled him like a branch on a tree. A massive whale dipped, rose, and swam on fins; spectators cheered and clapped. The boy collected images and recreated tenable abstracts after sunset. Before going to sleep, he thought about his grandmother. He craved her grape leaves stuffed with lamb meat and rice. She baked the best homemade Herisa topped with skinless almonds. She made her cookies with goat milk, raisins, and crushed

وَلاَ تَحْسَبَنَّ الَّذِينَ قُتِلُواْ فِي سَبِيلِ اللهِ أَمْوَاتًا بَلْ أَحْيَاء عِندَ رَبِّهِمْ يُرْزَقُونَ

pistachios. She made her salad with thirteen different fruit, vegetable, and her famous dressing.

ALLAH cleared the path for his wish. Snow brought peerless dreams and planted a new rose in his soul. Romance with snow, his second sacred love after his religion, paved a road of no end. If he had the power of Prophet Dawood pbuh, he would call on el-Hutaib village to come to him and bring along a flight of Hoopoes so all can sing "O' Canada."

He never can forget the first home on Irving Avenue: Bungalows on both sides lined up like white castles or the train ride from Ottawa to Calgary. Yunus Nef'i loves thick flakes falling in a hurry from an entirely peaceful sky; he feels like an angel, not needing water, food, or sleep.

He fell in love with Ottawa's snow that November day before he and his family got off the train on Wellington Street. A new Ottawa home, with five feet of snow, promised a daring life filled with surprises.

Years swept his youth and climbed over his old age. The dream house that brewed, half Yemeni, half Canadian, happened. The sun, a kiss from a large foyer window, shines at the large crystal chandelier, the cathedral ceiling, and the walls.

On a snowy night, he fasted; only air entered his mouth. He controlled his urge for tea, lebni and pita bread. Flakes falling on the window spiked his craving for dates and pomegranate juice.

Trees wore a bride's veil, which reminded him of villagers in gowns with white braids around the waist and sleeves. Telephone poles stood naked, old with bruised skin, sad, unable to hold the flakes.

Yunus leered at the precious images and filled his eyelids with thin pieces of snow. Anxious moments fell for his brush; he sketched with his pen, painted with his lashes, his soul in his palm mixed and matched the colours. Ottawa grabbed half his heart, left him the other half, parked in the middle like a bridge between two souls.

It takes nine months of pregnancy for little white saints to fall, bypassing the sun and leaving it behind. Yunus stood by the bow window on the second floor, glued his eyes to the view. White skirts braced homes, and

وَلاَ تَحْسَبَنَّ الَّذِينَ قُتِلُواْ فِي سَبِيلِ اللهِ أَمْوَاتًا بَلْ أَحْيَاء عِندَ رَبِّهِمْ يُرْزَقُونَ

whipped diamonds stacked on roofs. Branches dipped in yogurt numbed his palms, his chest expanded; a breeze rushed into his lungs.

He hoped to ALLAH the scents do not break his fasting. Seventy-five years have passed; he still pictures the flakes in the Gatineau Hills like torn jasmines.

He turned a small space on the second floor facing the foyer bow window into a cozy den; a granite-top desk sat inside the u-shape walls of glass bricks thirty-six inches high. He tugged a custom wall unit in a corner to the left, adjusted his favourite La-Z-Boy leather chair to his height, and set the levers to lock and rock.

He kept his desk surface clear except for his notebook, computer, notepad and pen. He felt a weird vacancy in the brain but not in the heart. Soul and heart united in a majestic span and freed his pen. The little white saints multiplied, arrested the entire sky, and gave the Earth a wedding no orbit saw in a million years. He rolled back in his chair away from the keyboard to get a better view. Passion borrowed his hands, pierced through the window, caught some flakes, held them in his palms and squeezed until all melted.

He pressed on the keyboard with wet fingers and tuned lines as they appeared on the screen. He never spoke in his inner voice and didn't leave his chair. The whole poem took a nap. Pages absorbed ink quickly to prevent smearing and cuddling together.

He remembered the Port of Montreal, the train ride, and the images of Irving's homes. He only realized how many decades had passed when he looked at the high ceiling. He kept his eyes on the foyer window while a storm of thoughts and metaphors flooded his mind.

Snowflakes tethered his tongue, arrested his emotions, and touched his face like air blades scoured his skin. He envies trees of white jewels, homes of silver crowns, and mountains of crystal peaks. He envies fields and hills of the whipped soft diamonds and all that leaves him out.

Envy is nothing compared to his anger, as vehicles of all sizes kill with every tire turn. Joggers and ordinary walkers, too, kill the flakes with each

وَلاَ تَحْسَبَنَّ الَّذِينَ قُتِلُواْ فِي سَبِيلِ اللّهِ أَمْوَاتًا بَلْ أَحْيَاء عِند رَبِّهِمْ يُرْزَقُونَ

step; machines clear the streets like vacuum sniffing evidence at a crime scene.

Snowflakes return to their wombs in Heaven, and Yunus Nef'i waits for the next season. He checks the calendar on the wall like a prisoner and bottles the social elegy he accumulates between March and November. Energy dwindles. He catches his breath and recuperates quickly. Flakes love trees more than stars love skies. Leaves in crystal gloves sway; branches in lingerie up to shoulders pose to the soft, gentle breeze.

Metaphors cannot justly speak of this wedding or imagine a honeymoon of this romance. No language has sharp teeth to unlock or shield this love story.

Yunus Nef'i despises all means that squish flakes under wheels. Boots step on them; bulldozers push them, trucks dispose of them, and winds scatter them. But mother nature weaves them: Valleys get spreadsheets; fields get carpets; mountains wear white crests.

The white miracles resurrect from a tissue, descend to the Earth, coalesce with oceans and rivers, and ascend in seamless vapours. They decorate the skies with jasmine lips, kiss the air, tease the clouds and enter wombs and brew; resurrect and fall; touch everything under the sky; earn martyrdom when cleansing the air, quenching the Earth, and land in oceans, lakes, and rivers. Earn martyrdom, when melting in children's hands, earn martyrdom every time they fall and return.

Ottawa hosts thirteen snow queens. Yunus merges night into day, in love with snow. Jealousy will kill him one day. Night shrivels; he hides in his den; he lends his eyes to a dream, writes down his thoughts, and his soul baptizes the lines before returning them to his heart.

Dawn wakes: He writes a new poem and flirts with the cold wind while the snow decorates the air with diamond mush. Streets and sidewalks celebrate until the night sleeps, and trees undress when the sun's heat touches their skin.

Warm fingers press the keyboard like piano pedals punching notes. Yunus reminds himself every season to forget about the white city and return to the red-hot soil in his village, roasting in the boiling grains until cured of all

وَلاَ تَحْسَبَنَّ الَّذِينَ قُتِلُواْ فِي سَبِيلِ اللهِ أَمْوَاتًا بَلْ أَحْيَاء عِندَ رَبِّهِمْ يُرْزَقُونَ

evil spirits. But as soon as snow fever hits his spine, and he realizes snow and rain do not fall on el-Hutaib village; he asks the season for forgiveness and will never do it again.

Ottawa cannot stop the snow; his pen and soul stand on guard for thou and thee; his pen and soul sing spiritual hymns like a heart in a baby's chest. Poetry evened the scale between a fight for justice and a corrupt world. Yunus never seriously thought of leaving his city, but he wants el-Hutaib village to remain always the rose he raised inside his soul to live forever. He regrets his health condition does not allow him to visit. But the wish inside his heart, clothed in Yemeni air, permanently sits where it chose ninety years ago. He carried that wish with him to Montreal. He gathered his emotion and passion for snow in a poem:

At first glance, I thought
the whole sky crashed,
I ran to the solarium,
dropped on the old couch
and released my eyes.

White carpets cover roofs,
decorate trees, embroider
and stitch the leaves,
children in snowsuits
play until red in the face.

Ottawa prefers snow over tulips,
trees glow, vehicles roll,
slide and swirl over icy roads
like ladybugs
dancing to Native songs,
snow unplugs my emotions
from my chest like Jasmine
leaving Damascus' soil.

Snow torpedoes exile,
my pen gains energy,

وَلاَ تَحْسَبَنَّ الَّذِينَ قُتِلُواْ فِي سَبِيلِ اللهِ أَمْوَاتًا بَلْ أَحْيَاء عِندَ رَبِّهِمْ يُرْزَقُونَ

pages absorb thoughts
before readers,
snow recharges life,
death respects the relationship,
snow, for me, is "love at first sight."
I am not the only admirer:
Birds land on trees
cuddle on skewers
covered with diamond beads,
the tourists visit each season,
depart when the feathers warm up.

I move to the driveway,
watch life engaged,
joy and peace dance
like air trapped
in a cola bottle.

With tight lips, many thoughts
pass and return,
eyes glue to images
cannot stop time,
trees wave farewell,
spring promises
a new breed of roses
and flowers.

I learned
the secrets of Snow:
Flakes form in Heaven
for nine months
always acid-free,
marinate in holy milk
until becoming white.

وَلاَ تَحْسَبَنَّ الَّذِينَ قُتِلُواْ فِي سَبِيلِ اللّهِ أَمْوَاتًا بَلْ أَحْيَاء عِندَ رَبِّهِمْ يُرْزَقُونَ

The Seventh Sky's womb
delivers the flakes
in various shapes and cuts.

They arrive gracefully,
hang from trees
like crystal fingers.

I watched through
the large foyer window,
stars glimmer,
the moon shines
in a clear sky,
night and snow
are lovers,
hold hands
when the moon naps,
caress and kiss
until dawn wakes.

Flakes dip,
dance, rise and drop
with the wind,
decorate trees
in diamond chips,
cuddle on rooftops
like magnates on steel.

My eyes and pen
access the world of snow,
explore and build thoughts,
even the abstract shines
like a sparkling star.

The distinct season
fills my heart,

وَلاَ تَحْسَبَنَّ الَّذِين قُتِلُواْ فِي سَبِيلِ اللهِ أَمْوَاتًا بَلْ أَحْيَاء عِندَ رَبِّهِمْ يُرْزَقُون

warms it in tenderness
and joy,
gives me protection
as the skin on flesh.

I suffer during
the three other seasons
from shivering to near death.

But the Spring touches
my heart
when bees gather
on Parliament Hill,
or when I meet
my friend
on Sparks Street
every Sunday morning:
Professor Omar feeds the birds,
I read a poem out loud.

I struggle to stay alive
for the sake of snow,
poetry and my city.

In November,
I first touched snow,
started my first book
in November,
Melaka and I met
in November.

One eyelet of the scale,
evens my love for Melaka,
the other eyelet evens
my passion for the snow.

وَلاَ تَحْسَبَنَّ الَّذِينَ قُتِلُواْ فِي سَبِيلِ الله أَمْوَاتًا بَلْ أَحْيَاء عِندَ رَبِّهِمْ يُرْزَقُونَ

CHAPTER ELEVEN

Canada, the Museum of sixty cultures offers fresh seeds for a poem, a sculpture, a tune, a brush stroke, or a chisel shard. Here coast to coast, the past, the present and the future meet. Yunus Nef'i writes a dozen poems in his head; his memory holds a collection; infinite space around him and beyond the beyond liberates his pen to roam anywhere and back to his den or his favourite café, coffee still warm. He cannot write in a confined environment unless right in the path, and poetry the road.

All living things begin from water, poetry included. A desiccated brain cannot digest a thought or respond to a heart, soul, or an impatient page. In his perceptive years, he realized emotions lead the spirit to the unknown.

What ignites the spirit to travel in supersonic speed and return before an eyelid close? Seventy-five years of memories, youth to old age brought Yunus Nef'i to a conclusion: Shadow Energy drives the spirit. The science of today or in the future cannot explore, understand, or handle the most esoteric knowledge in the Universe.

He believes in the loyalty of spirits; his pen, eyes, heart, and soul grow in his inner self as a baby in his mom's shadow. His spirit travels on the Y5 path of a sort. A peaceful dialogue enters his heart like a holy verse. His spirit takes him to el-Hutaib village and gives him a tour inside his home. He travels with his grandmother to their grapevines or watches his father work in the one-room sawmill.

On his first day in Canada, he pictured a journey full of surprises. Canada warmed up her bosom and welcomed him, unlike el-Hutaib's arms. He felt her hugs; love streamed from her palms; the first night on her land, he dreamt he was a baby inside a womb of veins stretching for thousands of miles.

وَلاَ تَحْسَبَنَّ الَّذِينَ قُتِلُواْ فِي سَبِيلِ اللهِ أَمْوَاتًا بَلْ أَحْيَاء عِند رَبِّهِمْ يُرْزَقُونَ

Canada's vast land seemed a good fit for his endless dreams, especially when he thought of his small village. He realized a home could be anywhere where justice and freedom exist. He loved Ottawa with a passion; poetry opened doors to new visions. On the first day, he gave his feet to Bank Street boutiques owned mainly by Lebanese immigrants—dining lounges and cafés north to south between the Confederation Building and Billings. He chose a different café each night, wrote poems, and always had a steaming coffee cup next to his pencil case. Nova, his favourite spot, breathed poetry.

The thirteen-year-old Yunus landed a job on his third day in Ottawa and secured a small apartment and basic living for his mom and siblings. He realized how much life differed in Canada compared to many Asian, African, and Arab countries. Canada offers the rich and the poor a chance to build a life. It provides education until pre-university, pays the poor and needy social benefits, pays for health care, and includes a child allowance.

Canada could become heaven dropped from the sky if the government, settlers, and immigrants gave her Natives an equal chance. If that happens, Yunus Nef'i will drop his most pious wish for a grave in el-Hutaib village and accept Canada's soil as a resting place.

A new phase dropped the curtain: Mom, brother, and sister died. Before he left Yemen, his dad died; the horror of war occupied his life. He wrote several books about how hate and bigotry altered human genes, abused nature in many ways, ended millions of lives, and left loved ones in deep grief for a very long time.

Caring for the family at a young age and guided by the Holy Qur'an eased his grief; patience guarded him against mischief; peace enlightened his soul. Poetry and philosophy uplifted his spirit. He discovered his passion for poetry while in the village he loved and considered a little heaven.

During his short years there, the power of metaphors, pencil, and paper allied with him. Grandmother triggered his journey to the world of poetry.

Her blue, blue eyes
shine on rosy cheeks,
nose, lips
and chin—all sit on

وَلَا تَحْسَبَنَّ الَّذِينَ قُتِلُواْ فِي سَبِيلِ اللهِ أَمْوَاتًا بَلْ أَحْيَاء عِندَ رَبِّهِمْ يُرْزَقُونَ

on a slender neck;
hair drops
like threads of pure honey;
each time
I look in the mirror,
I feel her hands
touching my face.

He recalls her stories about snow and how a wish in a dream urged him to live with her in Lebanon, but that never happened. He thought about her the minute he put his head on the pillow. He wished death would not take her until he graduated from university, got a job, married, and had children.

His children lost the chance to play in her backyard and eat cookies. She died in Lebanon before he left Yemen. He carried her memories past the seven seas in the most accessible sector of his brain. Occasionally, he hears her talk about Mount Haramoon and Mount Lebanon in winter, "The flakes fall evenly from peak to bottom and spread to the valleys. In the early morning, the sun umbrellas Mount Haramoon; at dusk, it descends and kneels graciously before Mount Lebanon."

Yunus Nef'i discovered humanity's true meaning from his dad, who carried carpentry tools in a box, on foot, to various towns and villages. Half of the earnings took care of family needs; the other half went to Zakat.

During his years in Canada, he realized a poet's commitment to poetry resembles dad's sacred obligation to people experiencing poverty, but the distribution differs.

A poet's petite royalty pays for ink and paper; any change left pays for bird seeds. Other forms of Zakat toward land and honour deserve struggle and sacrifice forever.

Palestinians have donated blood for honour and freedom since the beginning of time. Every civilization fought over el-Quds, the holy capital of Palestine. Palestinians fought back, suffered under each occupation, gave martyrs, starved, lived in poor and inadequate shelters, and tolerated prison torture but continued donating blood.

وَلاَ تَحْسَبَنَّ الَّذِينَ قُتِلُواْ فِي سبِيلِ اللهِ أَمْوَاتًا بَلْ أَحْيَاء عِندَ رَبِّهِمْ يُرْزَقُونَ

In 1948, the Zionists killed half the Palestinians and expelled most of those who stayed. If the British didn't wait around, the Zionists would have murdered every Palestinian. The British stayed around, so the hatred they created continued.

Today, the Zionists exercise various methods to see Palestinians under occupation, and the ones living inside the Green Line perish. War on Gaza flattens homes; F-16s return, and bomb after Palestinians rebuild. Army tanks kill children because they throw rocks; settlers burn plantations and pollute fishing water to starve fishers and farmers. The Zionists control drinking water, food, electricity, medicine, and checkpoints to the outside world.

Despite Europe and the U.S. behind Israel and dictators in the Middle East following on fours, the apartheid state realized Palestinians' struggle survives in and under fire, on the ground and in the deepest oceans. For every martyr, Palestinian mothers deliver ten newborns.

A load of emotion sits on Yunus Nef'i's chest. Palestine's chains ate her skin, the flesh, and the bones. Words drain his energy and pierce his heart. He remembers the boy who threw a rock at an Israeli tank and got back a round of shells that shattered his shoulder and arm.

Injustice imprisons words; occupation broils like steel in a pot of fire; wisdom and courage flow like a river; emotions scorch heart and singe the blood; letters curl and cry—pages cringe. The boy continues throwing rocks with the other arm.

Yunus wants to reach the rock thrower's soul, meet the mother who nourishes him, and build his steel body. ALLAH favoured Palestinian mothers with Heaven's pure milk: One fountain laces to the wombs; the other attaches to the breasts. A small rock in the palm of a Palestinian boy or girl weighs a ton when it falls, the arm like a rocket launcher. Yunus Nef'i tries hard to describe the images, but words fall off the page; eyes tear for the drop, ears drums pucker, metaphors bulge; grief escapes— disgruntled with humanity.

Science lied about the steel forms from minerals inside the Earth. ALLAH sent down a shiny bronze liquid straight to the Seventh Earth. Half the

وَلاَ تَحْسَبَنَّ الَّذِينَ قُتِلُواْ فِي سَبِيلِ اللّهِ أَمْوَاتًا بَلْ أَحْيَاء عِندَ رَبِّهِمْ يُرْزَقُونَ

bronze mass regulated the orbit's rotation during the process. The other half thickened inside wombs, brewed, and dissolved into dust. The wombs of the Seventh Earth gave birth to minerals. Mother Earth turned them into steel. Palestinian mothers' milk goes through the same formation.

Young Palestinians rest on their blood; Israeli soldiers leave the scene quickly and take great pleasure in killing. What womb carries a hateful breed devoid of emotions and feelings? This breed walks on two feet but carries the blood of pigs and the genes of monkeys.

Israeli soldiers and settlers ridicule the rights of Palestinian children to live like other children. If they lived in derision, devils would show mercy toward youths defending themselves with small rocks against tanks. There exists no force on our planet that can beat these youths. Palestinian mothers deliver babies faster than an assembly line, readily conditioned to confront tanks with rocks. The Zionist occupiers realize a humiliating defeat awaits them, so they kill and destroy mindlessly.

O' Palestine, ALLAH gave you soul and veins as long as the Nile. Adam recited Ethan in your right ear. Hawa named you Filestine. Enemies fought for thousands of years to capture you for good but failed. The Romans and others perished. The UK crashed. Self-destruction began to slice the body of Israel. You lie down with cuffed feet and arms; concrete walls block the morning sun. A holy Rainbow will shine on your land; the sun will peel ribbons from her amber skin and decorate children for bravery.

Settlers uproot trees, shoot sheep and goats, and elders plant veggie seeds. Helicopters spray the fields with sodium carbonate. O' Palestine, step on the heads of foes with your mountain-feet and hold forever.

Zionists believe olive trees walk and talk. Branches hide deadly spears like a Jambiya in a sheath. The Stone-throw of a young boy or girl drops like a roof fall. Stone throwers chase tanks: Soldiers live in fear; mountains produce rocks; olive trees raise branches; olive trees do not sleep; olive trees pose as ghosts. Mothers deliver babies; children stock on rocks; Israelis live in fear. Children frighten the occupier more than a knife over the neck of a settler chained hands and feet.

وَلاَ تَحْسَبَنَّ الَّذِينَ قُتِلُواْ فِي سَبِيلِ اللهِ أَمْوَاتًا بَلْ أَحْيَاء عِندَ رَبِّهِمْ يُرْزَقُونَ

Seven skies guard el-Aqsa Mosque. Zionist bugs and Donald Trump believe they can destroy the holy Site. Holy Air holds the Holy Rock inches above the ground. A messenger of the angel species will deliver the deed certificate to the mailbox of the holy Shrine. When the Holy Rock finally sits, the holy Gravity returns to Heaven, and Palestinians and Torah Jews will know their natural origin and roots.

Palestine moves from Yunus Nef'i's mind to his heart and flows into all his being. He fills a pen swathed with tears; when he reads a Palestine poem, an incredible shine forms a bright sheen on his face.

When Israel fires smoke bombs to darken Gaza's sky, the ray of Palestine shines on the ground like fields of candles.

Nations that believe in miracles should clone the bloodline of Palestinians or Torah Jews and study the history of Palestine's pre-human existence.

Zionists control checkpoints: Release small food and water when tired and drained out, none when sober. Palestinian children starve and eventually die, and ten new babies spring out for every death. What gain did the Zionists achieve? Sleep in fear and wake with the same fear. Zionists had not had one minute of peace - - not before or after confined Palestinians inside walls a hundred feet high and miles long. Zionists rejoice when F-16s mince children, women, and elders. If the sun changed places with the Earth, the skies would turn to flipped oceans that can not hold back the Predetermined Promise of freeing Palestine.

Palestinians live the injustice imposed on Prophet Yusuf [pbuh] and endure the Pharaoh's oppression forced on Prophet Musa [pbuh.] Prophet Yusuf [pbuh] became the Trustee of the Earth's treasures; Musa's staff split the Red Sea and saved his people. The sea swallowed the Pharaoh's army. Locusts, weevils, frogs, and virus plague delivered death punishment to his followers and turned them into deflated corps.

The Israeli Army evicts families from homes they owned five thousand years before the time of King David. The issue is not who lived in Palestine first but who extended the olive branch. Yunus reflects that in a poem:

وَلاَ تَحْسَبَنَّ الَّذِينَ قُتِلُواْ فِي سَبِيلِ الله أَمْوَاتًا بَلْ أَحْيَاء عِندَ رَبِّهِمْ يُرْزَقُونَ

O' descendants
of Prophet Ibrahim pbuh
return the land
to Palestinians,
share their home,
food and water,
live with them forever
under one sky
on one land side-by-side.

Water and groom
olive and fig trees,
rebuild Haifa's orange plantations.

Plough the field
and harvest the crops,
bake the bread
and milk the goat.

Make Baklawa
and Rosh Hashanah,
dance the Hora
and Debkah.

Leave all borders open
so neighbours can visit,
and you return the visits
with baskets of olives,
fresh grapes and figs.

Ship nukes
and F-16s
to Donald Trump,
tell him:
We solved the feud for good,
no yellowed-hair Shaitan
should decide our fate.

وَلاَ تَحْسَبَنَّ الَّذِينَ قُتِلُواْ فِي سَبِيلِ اللهِ أَمْوَاتًا بَلْ أَحْيَاء عِندَ رَبِّهِمْ يُرْزَقُونَ

You lived in Arabia
from the river
to the sea
for thousands of years,
yes, then,
was family friction,
but neither side
evicted the other.

Flush Zionism in the toilet,
you need each other
as roots wait for rain.

The Arab Spring speaks
in your voice, stars
shine on your path,
the sun rewinds your energy,
follow your heart,
separate only when death
claims your souls.

The Arab Spring just turned twelve; complexion marks construe all cultures; speaks all languages; holds Adam's genes and Hawa's innocence. It has Idris's wisdom and Noah's faith. It carries Musa's power, Ayoub's patience and Isa's holy insight. It wears Muhammad's divine virtue and Omar's spiritual verity.

Zionists want Palestinians wiped out. Palestinian mothers deliver one thousand babies daily; each baby is Palestine in skin, flesh, and soul. Nothing can stop this baby rush! Patience and faith unite; children bond with rocks. Zionist soldiers shiver.

The Arab Spring is a prophet no one can see; no one can predict her mission. Yemenis call her Bint el-Khither. Syrians call her Bint thil-Khernine. Tunis and Egypt honour her coming. Muslims say she gave birth to Palestine. Zionists say she trains Gaza fighters. Yankees deny her existence. Arab dictators shiver at the mere mention of her name.

وَلاَ تَحْسَبَنَّ الَّذِينَ قُتِلُواْ فِي سَبِيلِ اللهِ أَمْوَاتًا بَلْ أَحْيَاء عِندَ رَبِّهِمْ يُرْزَقُونَ

Obama betrayed the Americans when he turned into a Mullah. He created a terrorist group to kill Iraqis and Syrians and attack Turkey. Trump gave Israel more support than all U.S. presidents since the creation of the apartheid state. Zionists believe Trump can stop the Arab Spring: Lo behold, they know not: Trump plays politics, not to lose. Before entering politics, bankers fell on their knees. They are the creditors, and he is the debtor.

As soon as Trump realizes the Arab Spring is a million times stronger than America, he will rescind his decision el-Quds, the capital of Israel. He will move to Palestine, pray five times daily and join the camps of Torah Jews and Palestinians, cut ties with Arab traitors and lobby for the deportation of all Zionists.

And if Biden or Putin happens to come his way, he will alert the Gazans to come and grab them. Strange as it seems: He is the man who, privately or publically, cannot speak without slurring and slandering Arabs, Muslims and immigrants in general.

وَلاَ تَحْسَبَنَّ الَّذِينَ قُتِلُواْ فِي سَبِيلِ اللهِ أَمْوَاتًا بَلْ أَحْيَاء عِندَ رَبِّهِمْ يُرْزَقُونَ

Yunus speaks in a poem:

Pencil
writes and draws,
words speak,
images scream,
poems and portraits
depict ruins, death,
bones, no flesh.

Babies smother
in debris,
poems and portraits
touch no conscience,
break no heart,
no emotion shrivels,
or tears rub cheeks,
no hope seeps from the ribs.

Bigotry flows with urine,
cowardice follows
bowel movements.

Eye cries,
metaphors
beg for empathy,
baby limbs move
by an invisible force
and cuddle
with disfigured mothers.

Metaphors climb on walls,
walk-on sidewalks,
recite to trees in the company
of a compassionate reader.

وَلاَ تَحْسَبَنَّ الَّذِينَ قُتِلُواْ فِي سَبِيلِ اللّه أَمْوَاتًا بَلْ أَحْيَاء عِندَ رَبِّهِمْ يُرْزَقُونَ

A mountain dissolves in grief
when he hears the poems
and views the portraits.

Arab traitors
and Western leaders
thirst for blood,
carry hearts harder than a rock,
colder than the ice of Antarctica.

Martyrs drop Sijjil Rocks
faster than a hawk
racing down to snatch prey.

وَلَا تَحْسَبَنَّ الَّذِينَ قُتِلُوا فِي سَبِيلِ اللهِ أَمْوَاتًا بَلْ أَحْيَاء عِندَ رَبِّهِمْ يُرْزَقُونَ

وَلاَ تَحْسَبَنَّ الَّذِينَ قُتِلُواْ فِي سَبِيلِ الله أَمْوَاتًا بَلْ أَحْيَاء عِندَ رَبِّهِمْ يُرْزَقُونَ

CHAPTER TWELVE

Fate guided Yunus Nef'i to his favourite café when, in fact, he planned to pick up his computer at a repair shop located in the opposite direction, a dozen miles far. An African, sweet, old lady dressed in a red kaftan of pure wool sat in a chair, scarf wrapped around her shoulders and breasts. One glance at her pulled his emotions from his veins as he entered the door. Two elders meet in the same café after time stops for decades. He walked toward her; stared at the two cane-wood chairs, "I am Yunus Nef'i." She bashfully replied, "I am Melaka." Memory returned for both at the speed of the Y5, but both kept silent. Her coffee steam evaporated; no lips touched the rim. Silence sucked both into a crystal ball. The inner selves did not— lived the past, now reliving it again. A verse flashed in his head:

<blockquote>
She smiled, her stunning smile
grabbed my soul and lured me,
I experienced the glory of dying,
I searched for metaphors
to depict the braided hair
and the silver falls on her forehead,
the brows, the lashes, and the eyes
each shames rainbows and stars,
nose, lips, chin, and tattoos
on the cheeks require
an army of poets
and a mountain of metaphors
to portray her wisdom in a song.
</blockquote>

She set her eyes on him, palms wrapped around her elbows. A spark in her eyes shined on his ageing face. "You do not remember me?" she asked. "I typed your poetry collection in the sixties. We met here in this café in

وَلَا تَحْسَبَنَّ الَّذِينَ قُتِلُواْ فِي سَبِيلِ اللهِ أَمْوَاتًا بَلْ أَحْيَاء عِنْد رَبِّهِمْ يُرْزَقُونَ

November and sat at this table. I gave you a poem I wrote for a keepsake before I returned to Africa. You still have the poem?"

He looked at his watch. Fifty-nine years, seven hours and forty-four minutes passed. He stared at the table and looked around to ensure the café was the same. The same black and white TV hung from a ceiling corner. On November 18, 1964, angry patrons glued their eyes to the screen: J. Edgar Hoover, Director of the FBI, described Martin Luther King Jr. as the "Most notorious liar." Black and White Americans anticipated an assassination.

Yunus carried the poem she wrote; the one he wrote for her did not show to anyone and did not include it in his published books. He surprised her when he told her he wrote the poem before she typed his manuscript. He took both poems from his wallet, handed her the one she wrote, and said, "Please read it." Tears filled her eyes.

You write poems like a hen lays eggs,
metaphors pinched my thoughts
to the last verse,
tight chest and throbbing brain
hissing sounds and bubbling blood,
hot and cold fever
ran up to my head
and down to my toes,
your green eyes soothed
my heart like a prophecy,
you kissed my forehead,
my soul toured your whole being,
my eyelashes combed your hair:
If time lives to the end,
I still recognize you
in a crowd of a thousand men,
light in your eyes
destroyed the wall
that barricaded a song - -
your eyes played the maestro,

وَلاَ تَحْسَبَنَّ الَّذِينَ قُتِلُواْ فِي سَبِيلِ اللهِ أَمْوَاتًا بَلْ أَحْيَاء عِنْد رَبِّهِمْ يُرْزَقُونَ

your heart played the 12 notes.

Crystal tears softened Melaka's natural shyness. The white hair and the wrinkles added charms to the same smile of many decades. Emotion swept his face. Eyes lit up. He unfolded the poem he wrote for her and recited it:

Braided hair dropped on your back
like threads twisted in Sidr Honey;
each braid represented
one African nation;
I placed my palm on your forehead
and wished Heaven be our final place;
I walked under the shadow
of African magic;
Heaven's door opened;
fifty-four jewels in various colours
sat on your crown:
You walked toward me like a princess:
Your brows of the exact size,
shape and colour
guard two small islands
of emerald shades;
lashes open and close
like the mouth of a baby fish;
my eyes stared at your braided hair,
landed at the soft shores;
the two lids opened,
thoughts streamed like a breeze
carrying a miracle to a soul;
from there, I measured your beauty
with the pupils of my heart;
all dimensions equalled
the square root of your eyes;
each side of your cheeks
outlined the upper and lower lip;
my pulses throbbed, clapped
and veered toward you.

وَلاَ تَحْسَبَنَّ الَّذِينَ قُتِلُواْ فِي سَبِيلِ اللهِ أَمْوَاتًا بَلْ أَحْيَاء عِندَ رَبِّهِمْ يُرْزَقُونَ

Melaka held her tears not to disrupt his recitation. Each word fell on her like a raindrop. She pictured herself in a small garden and Yunus, a single cloud pouring rain. He continued his recitation:

The sun reflects on your face
and envies your skin;
two babymoons a day old
guard your eyes;
your smile
flashes a pair of dimples,
I see us living in Heaven
in a small home by a river–
palm trees
on both sides of the entrance,
branches greet us with a wave
as we approach the door;
tulips tie our home in a horseshoe;
bees extract the nectar and return to hives.

Their hearts and souls stayed in touch like the sun breaking dawn and awakening dusk. On November 18, 1964, in the café, their souls traded places. Melaka recalled the streetcar ride from Sandy Hill to visit a relative on Island Park Drive. She got off at the intersection of Irving and Wellington. She walked into the corner café, not knowing why. Her heart said, "Stay," her mind said, "Island Park is twenty-five blocks away."

The hostess escorted Melaka to the only vacant chair at Yunus Nef'i's table and asked if the beautiful lady could use the empty seat. Melaka sat down, flashed a shy smile and thanked Yunus. Their eyes interlaced in returning waves of confused emotions. Yunus read the last poem he wrote for his collection; Melaka sunk in her chair and offered to type his manuscript. She gave her heart and soul to him. On that day, her soul left for a second and returned.

Was it a coincidence she entered the café when she intended to get off at Island Park Drive? The driver stopped the streetcar when no one rang the

وَلاَ تَحْسَبَنَّ الَّذِينَ قُتِلُواْ فِي سَبِيلِ الله أَمْوَاتًا بَلْ أَحْيَاء عِندَ رَبِّهِمْ يُرْزَقُونَ

buzzer, and no one waited inside the glass shelter to get on. Yunus intended to pick up his computer at a shop miles from the café. Did his heart replace his mind while his hands steered the wheels? "Coincidence" or not, his "heart" did steer the car to the place meant to be. Her intuition and the streetcar driver's third eye followed the guiding light.

Yunus came across this proverb: "If you love someone and circumstances force her to go, don't lose hope. If she comes back to you, she is yours forever." The heartfelt saying makes a lot of sense. They traded souls at their first meeting. Souls only obey the Call of ALLAH. "A spiritual love that begins on the Earth continues in the Hereafter." That was what Yunus Nef'i's grandmother said.

Pure affection for each other propelled quaint love of a kind never existed before; bonded two strange hearts, separated them in body, not the soul. She typed his manuscript in one sitting of sixteen hours on November 19, 1964. Admiration and passion built word blocks inside her soul; twenty-two thousand words became the only spoken language of her heart. Not an ordinary love bonded their souls, but a miraculous force joined all their senses. Yunus and Maleka became twins in one spirit.

Their love was like a storm that locked itself for fifty-nine years; it popped at the forty-fourth minute of November 1, 2018. She taxied from the airport straight to the café. Her heart and the pulse of her soul assured her Yunus would walk through the doors. She sensed his hands on the steering wheel. Melaka returned to Africa on November 19, 2018, and died a few weeks later. Yunus learned about her death on January 19 of 2019. Melaka never married; Yunus violated no holy codes. His spiritual love for Melaka sits inside his soul forever. All love stories told and untold, published or filmed, romantic and heart-breaking, fell short of the soulful love for one another.

وَلاَ تَحْسَبَنَّ الَّذِينَ قُتِلُواْ فِي سَبِيلِ اللّهِ أَمْوَاتًا بَلْ أَحْيَاء عِندَ رَبِّهِمْ يُرْزَقُونَ

وَلاَ تَحْسَبَنَّ الَّذِينَ قُتِلُواْ فِي سَبِيلِ اللّهِ أَمْوَاتًا بَلْ أَحْيَاء عِندَ رَبِّهِمْ يُرْزَقُونَ

CHAPTER THIRTEEN

One spark of freedom set a torch on fire. Bouazizi, the peddler, earned little money, hardly enough to feed his family. If one of his six children missed dinner, he could not run to a fridge for a snack or a sandwich. Tunisian Bouazizi torched himself on December 12, 2010. The wagon peddler's suicide swept the world by storm. His torch travelled like a light in the sky, quickly becoming the most significant freedom season against oppressive regimes. He gave birth to the Arab Spring in January 2011.

Bouazizi did not have a fridge; Bouazizi, the torch; Bouazizi, the martyr, did not know he was a walking fire, low in wealth, rich in heart, fighting oppression in all genera.

The angel disguised as a peddler flew to Heaven, returned with a torch, and set the world on fire.

He never heard of Omar el-Mukhtar, Gandhi, Fidel Castro, Che Guevara, or Nelson Mandela. He did not write poetry and did not spray graffiti on walls. Pure Bouazizi, no deformed genes, cloned tongue, or a weak heart, he ended his life, leaving us a torch forever lit.

Tunis sat on torrid mines. Oppression and bribe spread like an oil spill. Police and the mafia paid Ben Ali a cut of the extorted money. The tyrant also robbed the country and stashed forty billion in foreign banks. He died, cloth cuffs tied to his hands and cotton balls stuffed in his nose. Foreign banks use an unwritten law which allows them to share a deceased dictator's stolen wealth with their governments.

The peddler on wheels pushed his cart from street corners to boulevard squares selling zucchini and squash, potatoes and other veggies, and fruit— his goal in life was to secure food and water for his small family.

وَلاَ تَحْسَبَنَّ الَّذِينَ قُتِلُواْ فِي سَبِيلِ اللهِ أَمْوَاتًا بَلْ أَحْيَاء عِند رَبِّهِمْ يُرْزَقُونَ

Shark mobsters and local police pushed him, robbed him, and beat him numerous times for his money, or he stayed off the streets. Bouazizi set his wagon on fire and pushed the wheels until both frizzled; his torch guided Tunis to freedom, reaching Egypt and spreading to Syria, Libya and Iraq, reaching Yemen, Algeria, Sudan, Lebanon, and Palestine.

His torch of two enormous eyes roams Arab land night and day, looking for traitors and dictators.

Bouazizi ended his life. The poor peddler, uneducated, not prophet, not a saviour of sinners, gave up living, so wrong, stops. Bouazizi torched himself and his wagon because he did not have the power of a prophet to stop tyranny. He knew ALLAH forbids suicide. He sacrificed his life for a universal cause. Islam teaches, "Intention of righteous deeds overrides the results of action." May ALLAH forgive Bouazizi and grant him Paradise.

Bouazizi's family's trait began in Yemen and spread to the Sahara Desert. His forebears go back directly to the warrior el- Barrak Noor, one of the great knights of "Bouazizi Tribe." The great knight loved poetry and wrote it.

Storytellers told tales about el-Barrak Noor's love for Princess Suead Bint Abdullatif Ibn Mohammad Beni Ghassan, a gifted artist who never studied art but produced a masterpiece at age nine. Princess Suead loved poetry more than art, but her hand and eye got used to her brush. Her paintings reached the four corners of the world.

el-Barrak Noor knew the princess through her paintings. Both exchanged love impressions in poetry and art without letting each other know. He cherished her artwork. Princess Suead lived his poems second by second, minute by minute. Neither presaged what Fate had planned for them. The sea and the simmering sand knew.

She dug an easel in the sand and spread her colours under the sun; the sea waves rushed to the shore.

He placed a 10X10 cherry wood board covered with camel skin on his knees and pulled a papyrus and pen from a handbag. A few meters separated them. Pen and brush spoke eloquent metaphors. The dense eyelashes of her brush

وَلاَ تَحْسَبَنَّ الَّذِينَ قُتِلُواْ فِي سَبِيلِ الله أَمْوَاتًا بَلْ أَحْيَاء عِندَ رَبِّهِمْ يُرْزَقُونَ

rolled on the canvas like a breeze kissing roses in a garden. Her Eyes imprisoned his heart. He waved with a Salam; she blushed; water and fire fell on her.

The warrior collected the poem as it sprung from her eyes and stunning face. He used emotions and eyelashes instead of a pencil: His eyes write; his heart shines on the words. He captured their love in a poem. The prince was stunned, speechless, but she felt his poetry with tearing eyes. She opened all the doors to her heart; emotions flowed from her face. His eyelashes and pencil stopped for a moment. He followed her shadow to the sea. She spread her wings and fins and dived.

The world will not see, hear or read about a romance like their love story. The present narrator cannot produce another story, even if the odds were one-tenth of a tenth in a million. el-Barrak sums up her love in chosen words like picking roses in a garden; he looks at her extraordinary beauty and recites her poem; she listens with her eyes and ears looking at the canvas to hide her blushed face and stop her tears. The sea and the sand lay silently, spread like a flat orbit, half beige, half blue, with no trees, valleys and mountains except sand and sea.

Strokes of a magical brush
separate colours,
repose
like a flipped dusk,
charcoal clouds
mask the sky
and refuse
to release the rain
unless the brush moves away
and obeys your hand.

Your brush and the clouds fight
like noble warriors,
the brush needs the rain
to capture the miraculous drops,

وَلاَ تَحْسَبَنَّ الَّذِينَ قُتِلُواْ فِي سَبِيلِ اللهِ أَمْوَاتًا بَلْ أَحْيَاء عِندَ رَبِّهِمْ يُرْزَقُونَ

the clouds think the brush wants
to steal the rain
and bring out the sun.

Your brush defeats the clouds,
rolls the strokes,
creatures cheer,
roses, flowers, and greens blossom,
half the canvas turns marine.

The undefiled beauties
float inside husks,
dance, and sparkle,
exalt in joy, rove, and swirl,
rise and dive like dolphins.

You mix images from a tray
of original colours,
I turn to the sea and say,
your brush scooped
all the secrets in one stroke.

The North Sahara's vision
guides your dreams,
the desert's haze
showers you with ruby dust,
your brush follows your senses,
you rise toward the sky,
fall back into the sea and rise,
you touch the sand
with delicate feet.

You hide your fins and wings
under your white blouse,
a crown on your head
drips like betels

وَلَا تَحْسَبَنَّ الَّذِينَ قُتِلُواْ فِي سَبِيلِ الله أَمْوَاتًا بَلْ أَحْيَاء عِنْد رَبِّهِمْ يُرْزَقُونَ

leaking morning dew,
you pass by my small camp
like a lit cloud on feet
painting, on the one hand
brush in the other:
With each coffee sip
my eyes steal a tint
of your beaming face,
your shyness melts,
the nectar turns pink and red,
swords of soft blades
guard two mini stars,
shine on apricot cheeks,
a super white scarf
around your gazelle neck
falls to the elbows,
the almond liner reflects
on the sclera of your eyes
then sweeps the brown irises,
the pupils' spark,
the shy diamonds
pull my eyes from their sockets
and leave me blind.

el-Barrak Noor offers his soul and heart; she counters with his vision, so she keeps the poem forever. He accepts the offer and says: "Keep the poem, the soul, the eyes and the heart."

He packs his deal inside his brain, handbag in hand, and sword buckled on the waist. He delivers his song passionately to ears under a black scarf. She holds her soft cheeks with both hands. Her smile glows as the moon sits on her head.

el-Barrak Noor cannot find metaphors befitting her cheeks, lips, chin, and gazelle neck. She stands to the height of a baby palm tree; shoulders levelled like a caravan of birds praying in space, wings folded. He continues reciting:

وَلاَ تَحْسَبَنَّ الَّذِينَ قُتِلُواْ فِي سَبِيلِ اللّهِ أَمْوَاتًا بَلْ أَحْيَاء عِندَ رَبِّهِمْ يُرْزَقُونَ

Your mom's cravings show
a cherry on one wrist
apricot, on the other,
an angel left kiss-imprint
on your forehead,
asked the LORD
to allow the wings to go,
take away the light-life
but grant permission
to stay with you:
The LORD elevates Love
above the highest ranks,
grants the angel's wish.

Your white blouse
falls to the waist,
the skirt drops
to the foot joints
embroidered in green
and red jewels
geometrically calculated
and spaced perfectly.

Your smile dims
the ray of the sun,
the sky never senses
a change.

The kiss on your forehead
and the angel's romance does not bother me.

He leaves the sand and the sea; she gathers all colours and brushes in a black leather portfolio and returns to her castle.

He walks toward the mosque, stops by a telephone pole, and hums a melody of her heartbeat: At the doorsteps of the Assalam Mosque, he falls on his

وَلاَ تَحْسَبَنَّ الَّذِينَ قُتِلُواْ فِي سَبِيلِ اللّهِ أَمْوَاتًا بَلْ أَحْيَاء عِندَ رَبِّهِمْ يُرْزَقُونَ

knees, calls the Shahadah, and dies on his right side, head in his palm. She hears about his death, scoops the sea with her eyes and sails away.

ALLAH created her of Mariam's purity, giving her Aisha's wisdom. The world will never see the beauty of her match or close, as HE destroyed the mould.

وَلَا تَحْسَبَنَّ الَّذِينَ قُتِلُواْ فِي سَبِيلِ اللهِ أَمْوَاتَا بَلْ أَحْيَاء عِندَ رَبِّهِمْ يُرْزَقُونَ

124

Actor Osman Soykurt played Ibn Arabi in
the world-renowned film "Ertugrul."

ولاَ تَحْسَبَنَّ الَّذِينَ قُتِلُواْ فِي سَبِيلِ اللهِ أَمْوَاتًا بَلْ أَحْيَاء عِندَ رَبِّهِمْ يُرْزَقُونَ

CHAPTER FOURTEEN

Rasheed Muhyi-eddying Ibn Arabi opened an eatery in 1925 and established the first children's birthday club for those aged 12 and less. The birthday child got a free meal, bells and whistles, cake, and candles. Rasheed never thought the Ottawa eatery he named "The Family Nest" would grow into a chain. By 1935, he owned one eatery in every major city in Canada and America. The Birthday child got free arrangements and a free meal, which generated revenues no ads could generate in a hundred years.

The founder died in 1936 while visiting Syria with his wife and only son. Son, Bilal, remained in Syria; he died on August 1, 1941—one year after his marriage to Aisha Beni Nehian, who delivered baby Omar on August 17, 1942.

Grandparents on the mother's side raised Omar and supported him until he graduated with a PhD in Arabic literature from Damascus University. Omar took a teaching post in the same faculty and then moved with his mom to his Grandparent's second home in Hama.

Omar Bilal Muhyi-iodine Ibn Arabi and Nusayba Beni Umran, born and raised in the same city, graduated from the same university. Nusayba and her mom also moved to Hama after her father died.

February 13, 1972, Omar walked Nusayba down the aisle; their feet warmed the marble floor; chandeliers of pure crystal hanging from the cathedral ceiling sparked on the rhythm of a grandfather clock. Guests danced like affectionate royals. They ended the evening like a story in a book: Love, peace, great food, a pile of gifts, original bone china, cookware and precious jewellery stacked on an antique credenza. They had their first baby on June 10, 1973. ALLAH gifted them five more from March 13, 1974, to February 1, 1982. One grandmother and two grandfathers died before the children were born.

وَلَا تَحْسَبَنَّ الَّذِينَ قُتِلُواْ فِي سَبِيلِ اللهِ أَمْوَاتًا بَلْ أَحْيَاء عِندَ رَبِّهِمْ يُرْزَقُونَ

The city of Hama woke on February 2, 1982, to the darkest, saddest day. Hafez el-Assad, the savage president, declared war against protesters who peacefully jammed the streets, asking for jobs and justice. The butcher's army slaughtered over forty thousand in weeks and jailed thousands. Tanks levelled a substantial portion of the historic city. The world stayed mute. Hafez continued killing, jailing, and torturing thousands of innocent Sunnis until his last day. He died on June 10, 2000. Son Bashar became president ten days later by a rigged election that gave him 97% of the ballots. The new tyrant introduced harsher oppression and corruption. Joblessness soared; inflation spread to all sectors; innocent people filled the jails.

On March 15, 2011, tens of thousands jammed streets in cities and towns in a peaceful uprising. Bashar's tanks welcomed the mutiny with bullets. After six months of peaceful revolt, people took up arms in the seventh month. The fighters scored one victory after the other, capturing three-quarters of Syria.

The world ganged against fighters except for Turkey and North African countries. Obama and Arab dictators expressed readiness to finance and arm the fighters before the camera. Behind doors, assured Bashar of unwavering support. Obama gave Putin the green light to the war in 2014. Russian bomber jets filled Syria's skies, levelled Aleppo and nearby cities, towns, and villages, and forced resistance and refugees into Northern Syria. End of 2015, Putin, and Farsi-Iran's militias recaptured 75% of the land lost.

After twelve years of war, the U.N. waits for the queue from the five permanent members; the five wait for the queue from the Zionist state of Israel. Obama's circuitous plans stopped Bashar from falling. Obama saw the secret files of America's crimes against humanity in the Middle East and elsewhere. The law professor knew the minute he became president, America's dark record became his. Instead of showing remorse toward the Syrian victims, he allowed the crimes to continue.

Omar and his wife lost six children in 2013 to the vicious war one day after a sniper killed his mom. They escaped to Turkey and settled in a small apartment in Istanbul.

وَلاَ تَحْسَبَنَّ الَّذِينَ قُتِلُواْ فِي سَبِيلِ اللّه أَمْوَاتًا بَلْ أَحْيَاء عِندَ رَبِّهِمْ يُرْزَقُون

Omar taught Arabic to undergraduate students. Nusayba took a job in a gallery. In 2015 they boarded a Turkish flight with other refugees destined for Canada. Omar and his wife settled in Ottawa. Sorrow burdened their chests with a ton of steel. Omar met Yunus Nef'i on Spark Street; they talked about the war in Syria and the murder of Omar's family. Yunus returned home sad and angry. He pictured six children in shreds all over bedroom floors; wondered if they were awake or asleep before being bombed. The last fuse in his body malfunctioned. He did not care if his heart stopped or death stood at the door. He wrote a poem.

I want the night to begin
and time to stop,
time's seamless skin
and night's dark face
destroyed my wishes - -
the sun never turns into ice,
the world needs a new order:
A squirrel sits for mayor,
rabbits for the police force,
raccoons assemble an army
to destroy all weapons
and stop destructive research,
compensate garish scientists
with a broom to sweep the streets,
bees crouch for judges,
ants perch for the jury,
white mare sits for the queen,
donkey sits for Prime minister,
mules serve as ministers,
skunks run the parliament,
birds provide postal services.

Lovers of Spark Street Mall, parents and children did not know the man sitting on the same bench beside Yunus Nef'i was Omar, the professor. They did not know he was the grandson of Rasheed, the founder of The

وَلاَ تَحْسَبَنَّ الَّذِينَ قُتِلُواْ فِي سَبِيلِ اللهِ أَمْوَاتًا بَلْ أَحْيَاء عِندَ رَبِّهِمْ يُرْزَقُونَ

Family Nest. The professor fed the birds several times and spent half the day sitting on the bench. Today Yunus Nef'i arrived earlier with a new poem to share with Omar.

From rags to riches,
riches to rags
life moves and stops,
riches to indigent
life sinks like a rock
or float like a fish,
misfortune brings rags,
I pause and light a cigarette:
A hound dog comes to the door,
hunger rattles its chain,
dogs do not knock on doors
of lords blinded in shame
and bruised pride, house of rags
spares a piece of cheese,
bread chips and a half cup of milk,
the dog kneels
before the small snacks,
eats and drinks the little dairy.

Luck switches rags with riches,
loonies grow and stack,
no rain falls on sunny days,
wealth fills the home,
the server sets the dining table
with flower vase,
silk napkins, cotton tablecloths,
and silver steak knives,
forks and dessert spoons.
The chef prepares the gourmand,
butler stands in the foyer:
A homeless come to the door,

وَلاَ تَحْسَبَنَّ الَّذِينَ قُتِلُواْ فِي سَبِيلِ اللَّهِ أَمْوَاتًا بَلْ أَحْيَاء عِندَ رَبِّهِمْ يُرْزَقُونَ

dressed in rags
from a penny store,
fear swirls inside a joyous chest:
Happy days may not last,
rags and riches come and go
and continue through the rotation:
I invited him and seated him
at the head table,
after a pleasant dinner,
dessert and Arabic coffee
he asked
for a shot of ZamZam;
I gave him a suit,
shirt, necktie, and hat,
gave him money to purchase
a used fridge and stove,
Mariam gave him the cash
she saved
to buy the entire collection
of her favourite poet
Jalal Eddine Erroumi.

Years went by, rags returned,
I aced the eighty-ninth year
frail energy and slow mobility.

The homeless returned,
knocked on the door
hair greyer,
holding a cane;
he gave back the suit,
shirt, necktie, and hat
and left two bags of cash.

No one knows when or where

وَلاَ تَحْسَبَنَّ الَّذِينَ قُتِلُواْ فِي سَبِيلِ اللهِ أَمْوَاتًا بَلْ أَحْيَاء عِند رَبِّهِمْ يُرْزَقُونَ

rags and riches
stop taking turns - -
no hint of insight to remember.

Rags and riches come and go
like oppression
at war with justice;
oppression comes and goes,
one day glory, wealth, and fame
another day, begs the shoes
for mercy.

Sparks Street was busiest on Sunday morning. Parents and children waited outside the eatery while a hostess recorded each party's number in a guestbook. Omar's soft white hair, well-trimmed beard, shiny green eyes, and soft smile attracted children and parents to his bench; he looked like a saint. Children gathered around to hear a new story narrated from his inbred imagination. Since Omar discovered Sparks Street Mall, he read hundreds of stories the children loved with a passion. Merchants of Spark Street believed revenues soared since the bearded man started feeding the birds and narrating stories to children. The Street earned notoriety after his grandfather opened the first eatery in 1925. The birthday club grew to twenty thousand members in Ottawa. Members in each other cities of Canada and the U.S. varied.

Omar only learned about his grandfather's chain months after he arrived in Canada. He also learned from the chain's lawyers his grandfather named him the single heir of one billion dollars in net worth. That does not include the operating capital of a hundred million. The chain's net profit before taxes fluctuates between 75 to 100 million annually. Omar instructed the lawyers to donate 20% of the net profit to refugees of all nationalities on Canadian soil and elsewhere.

At their request, Omar and his wife received five-thousand dollars per month from the vast wealth as a cost for food, accommodation, and other incidentals. The allowance continues to the surviving spouse and stops at the death of both. Their joint-will states: "Should Omar and his wife pass, the Family Nest Corporation and all its locations must be transferred in

وَلاَ تَحْسَبَنَّ الَّذِينَ قُتِلُواْ فِي سَبِيلِ اللّهِ أَمْوَاتًا بَلْ أَحْيَاء عِندَ رَبِّهِمْ يُرْزَقُونَ

favour of a charitable corporation approved by the Canadian Parliament to provide financial assistance to refugees everywhere."

Super Star Pinhani Darwish, wife and children, paid a surprise visit to Sparks Street Mall to meet the great Syrian storyteller. As usual, children surrounded the bench, Omar in the middle, narrating a story in his crisp accent. The Media, cameras, and reporters forced their presence, showing no privacy or respect to the Super Star or Omar. The Super Star earned world fame for his English/Arabic love lyrics (qasida). He licensed a tune from a Turkish archive dating back to 655 CE and blended the Blues 12-bar and the Jazz 32-bar; each verse a five-minute recited in the voice of Pinhani Darwish to Nahawand Taqsim.

Sparks Street's congestion forced Omar to abridge his story but injected enough guts and a unique twist on the theme. The story was about a Yemeni Sailor who discovered a beautiful land many millenniums ago. The Natives, then, lived in high hills and mountains to give peace to animals, birds, marines, and nature. Natives found the sailor unconscious on Manitoulin Island's shores by a maple tree with only his clothes.

The Yemeni sailor toured the nation from the deepest east to the furthermost west. After six months of the expedition, the sailor returned to Yemen and shared all the experiences and discoveries about the Natives' tradition, art, music, and food. Similarities between the Yemeni Nomad and Canada's Natives stunned the sailor. Years later, Chief Umhagana sailed to Yemen with her family and deputies. She brought half of a large tablet with an Arabic inscription that passed from chief to chief for thousands of years.

A Yemeni guide escorted Chief Umhagana to hundreds of historical sites. They found the missing piece in Jabal An-Nabi Shu'ayb. Both pieces completed each other after a separation of six thousand years. The tablet is certified as the origin of two nations. Chief Umhagana returned to her beautiful land with great news about the Canadian Natives' ancestors.

The children and parents left Sparks Street as it swelled with locals and tourists. The Super Star sat beside Omar, his wife to the right, and the children stood to the left. Pinhani Darwish thanked Omar for the generous charity he placed in trust for refugees fleeing to Canada and other countries.

وَلاَ تَحْسَبَنَّ الَّذِينَ قُتِلُواْ فِي سبيلِ اللهِ أَمْوَاتًا بِلْ أَحْيَاء عِنْد رَبِّهِمْ يُرْزَقُونَ

So right, are the ones who thought Omar was a saint? A true saint he was. Omar told the Super Star his ancestors go back to Muhyiddin Ibn Arabi, the philosopher and thinker no stranger to schools of thought worldwide. It turned out Pinhani knew as much about Ibn Arabi as Omar. The Super Star wrote his PhD thesis on the great philosopher's work. Pinhani told Omar he intended to select one of Ibn Arabi's nasheeds (hymns) to include in his next concert. He hopes to sing the Arabic nasheed in its genuine tashkeels on the Nahawand scale without an orchestra.

People of Sparks Street merchants and customers learned a refugee inherited his grandfather's wealth months after he and his wife arrived in Canada. They learned the couple lost six children and a grandmother in the brutal Syrian war. The donation story stunned all Canadians. Churches across the nation played a Muslim anthem in support of Syrian refugees. Their story occupied headlines and TV news. The couple's life chills hearts. Only a few people could walk their journey to the end. The Syrian couple witnessed the worst atrocities and abuse of innocent people but never capitulated, buckled, or broke down, not even when Farsi-Iran militias killed their six children and Putin snipers murdered Omar's mom. They lost their home and all their memories. The couple's inner faith and willpower go beyond a book or animated story.

Fate chose Canada for their final stop. Grandfathers' wealth of over a billion dollars could not shake their humbleness and unique humanity or lure them into lavish living. They were content to live the final days in a country among compassionate Canadians. Arab bigots of kin and skin abused and tortured Syrians; they did not allow them everyday work for food and water.

Nusayba stole Omar's heart at age six. The love birds met in the second grade; schoolmates dared them to kiss on the lips: One kiss of a mere second ignited a child's rare romance. Omar and Nusayba spent most of their time together. They would have written off the night if sleep were not necessary. Each time they met, they greeted each other in a sibling hug; their hearts pounded at the same rate. They prayed in the same mosque, climbed the same fig tree, picked olives, watered the jasmines in public gardens, and sold roses from street corners.

وَلَا تَحْسَبَنَّ الَّذِينَ قُتِلُواْ فِي سَبِيلِ الله أَمْوَاتًا بَلْ أَحْيَاء عِندَ رَبِّهِمْ يُرْزَقُونَ

Omar kept two poems from his childhood pal Nusayba. She found the poems in a book by his favourite poet, el-Moetanebbi but could not understand why he did that. Omar may have planned the time and occasion to give her the poems, but death conquered that goal on August 27, 2019.

Smooth, soft, and long blond hair
drops past her waist,
covers her chest like a scarf of gold,
Nusayba's face
resembles the sun of Aleppo,
two baby stars glow on her forehead
under two babymoons
lay in precision and exactness,
eyelashes match the hair
speak without a voice,
her soul defines her purity,
her lips give birth
to a beaming smile.

Her beaming smile sends me to paradise
and returns me in minutes - -
below her lovely nose
sits a birthmark
in the centre of the upper lip
like a black diamond,
a dimple in the chin,
smaller than the pupil of an eye:
The little diamond
and the sweet dimple
tease all my senses
my heart almost stops - -
when I imagine the soft light
in her eyes,
everything else in me dies,
but her smile revives me,
blood moves:

وَلَا تَحْسَبَنَّ الَّذِينَ قُتِلُواْ فِي سَبِيلِ اللهِ أَمْوَاتًا بَلْ أَحْيَاء عِندَ رَبِّهِمْ يُرْزَقُونَ

Pulse regulates the flow;
Nusyaba reminds me of Aleppo
before the war,
she lives in my heart,
Aleppo occupies my soul,
slim neck
sits on petite shoulders
confuses baby gazelles
as to which species
they do belong,
five feet eleven inches tall,
a queen when she talks,
syllables shame the lute
the master of all music,
she added a new artery
between her heart and mine,
our blood flowed
into one stream.

Nusayba painted murals with tears and colours. She and Omar walked through the ruins of Aleppo streets; saw bosoms and limbs hanging on trees. Her brush rolled strokes in reverse to prove eyes and lenses see half the truth. Eyelashes of her brush despise the half-naked lenses, hate the hands that crafted it, and reject the deception it depicts. A rare chemistry ties Nusayba and her brush together like a twisted steel rod.

Nusayba paints her strokes
from a dark view, the reflections
appear bright on canvas:
The subject is a woman inside
the shadow of death - -
from a short distance,
you see a body
under rubble and debris
except for the face - -

وَلاَ تَحْسَبَنَّ الَّذِينَ قُتِلُواْ فِي سَبِيلِ اللَّه أَمْوَاتًا بَلْ أَحْيَاء عِند رَبِّهِمْ يُرْزَقُونَ

she drew the face
with a crisp stare so real
if you pinch the cheeks,
the eyes move;
she drew
fragments of Putin's missiles
piercing the woman's breast,
a granite slab on her abdomen
covered her private parts,
her newborn in her arms
not known alive or dead
but eyelids are closed,
the severed legs at the knees
a few feet apart
if she could speak,
she would say,
humanity died millenniums
of years ago.

O' mother of Aleppo, rise,
smile like a martyr, glow
like the People of the Cave
who died for three hundred,
and nine more years,
returned to life
when ALLAH said, Wake.

Nusayba died in her little Ottawa studio on October 13, 2019; she died on her back by her paintings like a feather. Months earlier, Omar died on Sparks Street, sitting on his bench. Syrians who died at sea closed their eyes and slept through a dream about Prophet Yunis pbuh and the holy Whale. Sea sang a farewell ode, not expecting them to wake. They woke because the marine funeral was the road to Heaven.

If Obama were a whale and America a sea, fifteen million Syrians and ten million Iraqis would not have turned into distraught refugees looking for

وَلاَ تَحْسَبَنَّ الَّذِينَ قُتِلُواْ فِي سَبِيلِ اللهِ أَمْوَاتًا بَلْ أَحْيَاء عِند رَبِّهِمْ يُرْزَقُونَ

shelters. Several million would not die, millions would avoid injuries, and tens of thousands would not have faced physical abuse and torture in the most objectified prisons. The sea mammals forbid to eat the victims of oppression because water law does not allow it.

Putin, Obama, Bashar, the Mullahs of Farsi-Iran, Trump, and Netanyahu have rocks for hearts, diseased consciences, and dehydrated emotions.

Yunus Nef'i writes poems in his favourite café; metaphors float in wells of sorrow, offers the napkin his tears, his compressed ribs ache. Metaphors cannot stop wars. Poetry cannot force peace. But if we did not have Zionists, Obama, Bashar, Putin, the Mullahs of Farsi-Iran, Trump and four Arab traitors, love, friendship and justice would be the theme. Enough said about an impossible dream, Yunus Nef'i returned to reality and carved a new poem from his wounds.

Fire sweeps Syria,
red ashes,
sand and water meet,
the sky is one colossal eye,
the stars
send satellite signals,
the moon turns
into a garden of light,
the sun becomes
an amber rose,
night and day merge,
nature smiles,
angels disguise in trees
and tune their ears,
oceans and rivers rise,
half of the half
of the Earth
runs with the flood,
deformed Shi'ites
joined the invaders
become savage killers,

وَلاَ تَحْسَبَنَّ الَّذِينَ قُتِلُواْ فِي سَبِيلِ اللّهِ أَمْوَاتًا بَلْ أَحْيَاء عِند رَبِّهِمْ يُرْزَقُونَ

dysfunctional Sunni leaders
care for seats
not land and honour,
they follow America's queue
like addicted prostitutes.

Putin supplied Bashar with a hundred thousand barrels. Bashar murdered and injured one million. Obama never cared about the one million killed and wounded. He achieved the legacy Hitler failed to earn. Syria will survive as she survived all invasions and wars. The enemy severed her parts in every attack. If Syria were not the eye and soul of Islam, the enemy would idolize her jasmine, palm and olive trees and treat her people like saints. Yunus Nef'i reminds enemies in his following poem that no oppression, occupation or destruction can end Syria.

Many a time, enemies unplugged
her sea-size eyes,
new eyes grew,
many a time, enemies carved
her spaceship ears,
new ears grew,
many a time, enemies pulled
her tongue from the roots,
a new tongue grew,
many a time, enemies severed
her mountain legs at the thighs,
new legs grew,
many a time, enemies cut
her loving arms at the shoulders,
new arms grew,
many a time, enemies removed
her generous breasts,
new breasts grew:
Bashar, Putin, Farsi-Iran,
and militias
severed all her parts, left the abdomen

وَلاَ تَحْسَبَنَّ الَّذِينَ قُتِلُواْ فِي سَبِيلِ اللهِ أَمْوَاتًا بَلْ أَحْيَاء عِند رَبِّهِمْ يُرْزَقُونَ

and head attached - -
she rolled toward the severed limbs,
used them for crutches and walked - -
tomorrow, she shall recall
all refugees to return home,
shall charge her bosoms with love,
prepare jasmine potion,
dates and camel milk,
and feed and shower them with love.

On the fifth day of the fifth moon
of the fifth hour, a bright horizon
shall fall on all of Syria
like a sea of light.

Syrians will jam streets, desperate
for bread and water,
hunger burns appetites
like oil on fire,
guns, explosions
and chemical fumes
mask off the sky.

All know they could die or survive; all chant, "We have no one but ALLAH. " Will the leaders and the traitors who abused, killed, and expelled Syrians, Iraqis, Yemenis, Palestinians, and other Muslims elsewhere receive the Pharaoh's punishment? Again, Yunus replies: The fifth hour shall tick, and in the last second, Russia, Farsi-Iran, and militias will leave. On the fifth day of the fifth noon of the fifth hour, a tornado shall drill Bashar and Arab traitors to the Earth's bottom half. On the anniversary of Hamza's murder, they will rise in charred statues bleeding black blood. With shocking bullets, Bashar's soldiers shot Hamza, the first child martyr.

وَلا تَحْسَبَنَّ الَّذِينَ قُتِلُواْ فِي سَبِيلِ اللهِ أَمْوَاتًا بَلْ أَحْيَاء عِند رَبِّهِمْ يُرْزَقُونَ

CHAPTER FIFTEEN

Mohammid Abdul Latif Mustafa, a renowned Canadian artist, painted Professor Omar sitting on the bench, feeding birds, surrounded by young children under a peaceful sky. The Canadian National Gallery displayed the masterpiece in the Canadian and Indigenous Hall. Professor Omar spent much of his time on Sparks Street, caring for various birds, telling stories to youngsters, and spending time with his friend Yunus Nef'i. The artist donated the masterpiece to Heritage Canada and asked to make it accessible to every Canadian university, college, and city hall. Heritage Canada fulfilled his request but went further. It toured the masterpiece to all popular galleries in the U.S., Europe, Asia, and the Middle East.

Yunus attended Mohammid's exhibition in Istanbul to see the new masterpiece, a mural 36X36 (feet) mounted on a solid brass plate 1.75 inches thick, depicting "The Birth of Miser," a story by Yunus. The Crown Prince of a wealthy kingdom purchased the painting. He did not display it in any of his castles because of its size. The 2.5 mil dollar price tag occupied the news for months. It turned out the Prince's interest went beyond the painting. Six armed men kidnapped Mohammid and collected a five-million-dollar ransom but released an imposter.

The assassinators dissolved the body in acid and smuggled it out of Turkey. The Turkish investigators suspect the Prince's security aides carried out the murder, recovered investment plus a hefty profit. Istanbul witnessed an identical assassination in 2018 of Jamal Khashoggi.

Mohammid had taped the story and added a poem Yunus recited at the exhibition. The Middle East and North Africa we know today were icebergs near Horseshoe Island of Antarctica. The Earth made a sharp turn during

وَلاَ تَحْسَبَنَّ الَّذِينَ قُتِلُواْ فِي سَبِيلِ اللّهِ أَمْوَاتًا بَلْ أَحْيَاء عِندَ رَبِّهِمْ يُرْزَقُونَ

calibration. Mountains, rivers, oceans, forests and new ozone settled in the Afro/Red Sea region.

The sun nursed the sand from rising to setting. The Red Sea split from the Horn of Africa and gave birth to baby Sinai, Baby Sinai grew, became a mom, and gave birth to baby Miser. The Nile sprung from the jugular vein of Ethiopia and reached Miser through Sudan's northern border. Miser then was a small lifeless land in a vast desert. For unknown reasons, it became the precious jewel everyone wanted. Despite having nothing to offer except the desert and the Nile, millions of nomads of various ethnicities settled in Miser in less than a century. The vast empire of Ethiopia built massive dams, which trapped 65% of the Nile in a lake, 35% flowed into Sudan and Miser.

Yemenis, Sudanese, and Palestinians turned the desert jewel into a trade centre and popular tourist attraction. Farmers planted trees along both banks of the Nile; poets wrote Arabic parables of spiritual healing for every inner pain, composed love allegories in praise of marriage, and spoke against adultery, killing, defamation, greed, envy, and idols' followers. Scholars offered the curricula; teachers taught it in high school to magistrate level. Architects built schools, hospitals, libraries, galleries, and pyramids. Scientists developed filtering plants and waste incinerator systems that burned waste beyond ashes. Clean air, pure water, healthy food, and vegetable and fruit gardens turned Miser into a real Paradise.

Engineers built tunnels seven metres deep—all connected to a central dam. The Nile's water flowing in the tunnels has a device on each shaft to stop the flow. Burning deserts caused heavy condensation and vapour, which turned into water.

The new water flowed through the rads' platinum pipes and filled vast reservoirs connected to the main water supply. The system provided water for all general-purpose, including farming, without using a drop of the Nile. A brilliant engineering discovery created water out of water. Not only that, it did not disrupt Egypt and Sudan's share of the Nile.

Scientists discovered by a fluke new energy in solar fibre cells. They knew how to retrieve the power using cosmic waves similar to the current panels

وَلاَ تَحْسَبَنَّ الَّذِينَ قُتِلُواْ فِي سَبِيلِ اللّهِ أَمْوَاتًا بَلْ أَحْيَاء عِندَ رَبِّهِمْ يُرْزَقُونَ

or mirrors. The mystery of the cosmic signals remained unknown. Miser received ample energy to power a light bulb or a fleet of ships. The user only needed a transistor device that works like a power switch or a TV remote—inventions from the little toy to the super fleet filled government and people's needs.

Scientists have come close to understanding the distribution of the wireless energy of the Universe, but they are still zillion knowledge years away. Scientists gave Miser a world of no wires, usage restrictions, and no service fees. They developed an automatic generator of various sizes as a backup programmed to react to emergencies without human assistance. Scientists suspected multiple sources in the galaxy produced solar fibre cells.

One courthouse hosted the disputes. The sitting judges were the elected queen and king who settled contentions elders could not mitigate. Local elders of wisdom decided 99 % of all disputes. Royals served one term of three years.

In the middle of 2012, a miraculous turn for the first time in nine thousand years, Egyptians freely elected a ruler. Their dream lasted a year or thereabout.

Israel crushed hope for continued democracy. Egypt's minister of defence, the Zionist undercover, kidnapped the democratically elected president and placed him in solitary confinement.

After five years of torture, the prison doctor killed the elected president by lethal injection. The defence minister fulfilled the Zionists' demands, sold pieces of Miser for cash, and sold the gold mines for one-tenth of a tenth of a billion to Israel and the UAE. Arab traitors and Western leaders shield the new Pharaoh to ensure Egyptians remain penurious forever.

Miser's friends offer roses in one hand, dagger in the other. If Miser did not exist, the entire world would still be the orphan it was.

If Miser meant not to be, the Red Sea region and North Africa would be neighbouring Horseshoe Island of Antarctica and the Nile flowing in Heaven.

وَلاَ تَحْسَبَنَّ الَّذِينَ قُتِلُواْ فِي سَبِيلِ اللهِ أَمْوَاتًا بَلْ أَحْيَاء عِنْد رَبِّهِمْ يُرْزَقُونَ

It was Miser that inspired the tulips of Istanbul and directed the Euphrates River to follow from the eastern region of Turkey into Bilad El-Rafeedine, the place of the nuclei of all civilizations.

It was Miser that inspired the cedars of Lebanon and directed prophets to Mecca and el-Quds.

All prophets crossed her land, drank from her Nile, and ate her dates and olives.

Where is Miser today? Starvation stands at her door. The middle and upper class represents 15% of the one hundred million. Eighty-five million, on the verge of starvation, suffer from an inevitable death or prison. Yunus recites a special ode to himself:

> I long and yearn
> to see Miser on her feet
> without crutches,
> long and yearn
> to see her smile
> without a grin
> and laugh with no fear.

> A little sac of Miser's soil
> and a bottle of Nile's water
> all I want
> before I surrender to death.

Yunus Nef'i would not use a gun; he does not know how to avenge the murder of Egypt's elected president and the tens of thousands of innocent victims murdered and tortured in prisons. He retaliated poetically instead:

> A sculptor created
> a mini statue of the new Pharaoh,
> a production company,
> made two hundred million
> and placed one
> in every urine stall.

وَلَا تَحْسَبَنَّ الَّذِينَ قُتِلُوا فِي سَبِيلِ اللهِ أَمْوَاتًا بَلْ أَحْيَاء عِندَ رَبِّهِمْ يُرْزَقُونَ

A portrait artist sketched
the faces of those who
wronged the elected president,
a paper mill imprinted their faces
on toilet tissues
and guaranteed free supply
for two hundred years.

وَلاَ تَحْسَبَنَّ الَّذِينَ قُتِلُواْ فِي سَبِيلِ اللهِ أَمْوَاتًا بَلْ أَحْيَاء عِندَ رَبِّهِمْ يُرْزَقُونَ

وَلَا تَحْسَبَنَّ الَّذِينَ قُتِلُواْ فِي سَبِيلِ اللهِ أَمْوَاتًا بَلْ أَحْيَاء عِندَ رَبِّهِمْ يُرْزَقُونَ

CLOSING REMARKS

Farsi-Iran started the fire, and Obama supplied the fuel. Putin, a ferocious murderer, sucks his lips after each Sunni murdered. Trump unloaded a hurricane of discrimination; his saliva dried, his lips chapped, and his light-yellow hair thinned. Macron, one reptile of two faces, growls with a tongue several metres long. Boris calls for peace.

Bashar killed, expelled and jailed 65% of his people, and his dad Hafez rots in Hell. Khamenei leads the world in deception and derision. One butcher rules Israel; a dozen others disintegrate in graves. Soon, Arabia will crush all her shackles, infiltrators and traitors, for the sun of freedom only shines from the East.

Creative pain throbs; metaphors rock; ears stretch; gunsmoke blinds eyes. Explosion locks teeth and twists tongues. Soldiers of a pen, brush, chisel, or voice die by incineration, a saw or acid.

A new morning, a new challenge, coffee aroma filled the dining room. Yunus Nef'i stopped talking about wars at home. He never told his wife about Ibrahim, the survivor of nine murders in el-Arish bloodbath. Soldiers killed seven siblings, tortured the dad to death, raped the mom and trashed her body.

One cup of coffee did not clear his head; he placed the pot on a tray, grabbed his pen and raced to the den. Alone, coffee near him, his spirit delivers a vision of Ibrahim's mom standing by an olive tree, Mariam and baby Isa pbut sitting under a fig tree. Haze blurs Ibrahim's mom's sight, but her hazel-blue eyes shine like a star; she holds a quill in one hand and an inker in the other; her hijab shields her purity, and her quill sucks as much ink as possible. Mariam holds baby Isa to her chest, and saintliness pours on them

وَلَا تَحْسَبَنَّ الَّذِينَ قُتِلُواْ فِي سَبِيلِ اللهِ أَمْوَاتًا بَلْ أَحْيَاء عِندَ رَبِّهِمْ يُرْزَقُونَ

like a brush sweeping a canvas. Yunus stares at the beaming ray on the toddler's face. Baby Isa repeats the words he uttered to his mom at birth.

"Grieve not: Your LORD has provided a blessing under you. And shake the palm tree toward you; it will let fall dates upon you. So, eat and drink and rejoice. And if you see any people, say," "I have vowed for the Most Gracious a muteness, so I shall not speak today to any person" (16): 24-26 Qur'an. Mariam looked at Yunus without saying a word. Baby Isa sunk into her chest and watched all the stars racing toward the moon.

Mariam and baby Isa vanished; Ibrahim's mom followed in thin blue smoke. Yunus felt a mountain sitting on his head—he thought a bird's feather touched his hair.

One foot in the real world, the other touching the little mat in the foyer, his heart struggled to keep the lungs going; life pulled one arm, death pulled the other.

The soul settled the score; blood streamed at full speed. His spiritual self parted quickly.

He sat in his Lazy-boy chair, thinking about what kind of world we would have had Zionists not existed.

Sinai, the Nile's lungs, the heart of Mount Tur, and Tuwa Valley's soul, is the holy land the Zionists refused to enter unless the indignant people left.

But Torah Jews and Musa stayed in the holy land. The indignant gained the other half they missed. The Zionists waited in the wilderness of no man's desert for Uzair (their god) to return.

90% of Torah Jews believe Zionists ordained Uzair, their god, and Christians cloned the forgery in Jesus. "ALLAH forgives not the deniers of HIS ONENESS but may forgive all other sins" (5): 110 Qur'an.

Wavy hair meets the rhythmically combed beard and mustache. The dimmed wisdom shines in the green eyes. Yunus Nef'i carries a computer in a leather case; the side pocket holds a notebook, and the left a pencil. He ended his literary journey and wrote his last poem. He did not expect a story in a dream: A lady in space, not far from him, waved, unable to sustain a

وَلاَ تَحْسَبَنَّ الَّذِينَ قُتِلُواْ فِي سَبِيلِ اللّهِ أَمْوَاتًا بَلْ أَحْيَاء عِندَ رَبِّهِمْ يُرْزَقُونَ

consistent position. Fear in her eyes covered her face. He raced like an Ambulance, grabbed her hand, and said, "Come along." He rescued her after she missed the route to her home. She had many things to say but kept staring at his beaming face. His green eyes swayed her heart like a baby in a rocker. His wavy white hair and baby cheeks loosened all her joints. She thought she buried her heart under the hearth of her fireplace before she departed to the Better World.

The dream ended. Yunus sensed the space lady's feelings toward him—felt them in his heart, saying, "Romantic moments do not end with age, not in a dream or awake." This last story confirms dreams and reality are one mystery of two faces; one invades your sleep, the other flows in your wakefulness.

On the second day, he walked to the café, entered the doors and paused. Fear swept his entire body as he broke GOD's Rules. The space lady's ghost sat at his favourite table in one of the chairs. He froze, leaning on his cane. She thought he did die standing, ran over, and grabbed his arm. She helped him to the table and sat him down. She introduced herself, "I am Okwi." He raised his weak shoulders and shook his head. He tried hard to tell her he saw her in a dream floating in space wearing the same dress and crown, but his vocal cords and articulators ceased. Okwi's ghost vanished after forty-five seconds. Two selves abide in her body, dream, and spirit. Okwi either has a twin sister or lives two lives, one spiritual. Both scenarios validate Yunus' theory of the unseen, affect us, touch our hearts and leave us with unforgettable memories.

Yunus returned home, made himself aniseed tea and took a nap. He saw Okwi again in a dream: This time, they danced, talked, hugged and kissed on the cheeks, and shared Arabic coffee until the sun curtained the front window with sparkling rays. Okwi stole his heart by force. Melaka's face zoomed toward his eyes. Only after he woke, he realized the dream occurred and left.

He went for a walk with his dog, thought about a poem idea, rushed home and sat in his Lazy-boy chair, hands on the keyboard and eyes on the screen. Natives say the maple tree resembles the human mother, but the mother's

وَلاَ تَحْسَبَنَّ الَّذِينَ قُتِلُواْ فِي سَبِيلِ اللهِ أَمْوَاتًا بَلْ أَحْيَاء عِندَ رَبِّهِمْ يُرْزَقُونَ

nectar is sweeter and more delicious than the Sidr Honey of Yemen. Okwi's mom passionately craved maple syrup during her pregnancy.

Okwi's dense hair
reaches her waist,
shines like the brown nectar
and smells like foliage
of a Native maple tree - -
a crown embellished
in feathers and jewels
sits on her tiny head,
irises float motionless
over two mini oceans,
lashes guard against evils,
heart breathes through the pores
of blushing cheeks - -
beneath the daring brows
lies her Native history,
warm cheeks and bashful smile
intercept my attention
and imprison me:
I search for perfect words
to depict her overall beauty;
I find none; I ask my heart:
Emotions pour like heavy rain.

Freckles on arms and chin
add charms
to crimson cheeks,
reddish-brown blouse
barely seen, hides
under a black leather jacket,
red silk shawl
designed like a bib
drops over her shoulders,

ولاَ تَحْسَبَنَّ الَّذِينَ قُتِلُواْ فِي سَبِيلِ اللّهِ أَمْوَاتًا بَلْ أَحْيَاء عِند رَبِّهِمْ يُرْزَقُونَ

displays woven colours
in yellow,
orange, crimson
and scarlet - -
her long blue skirt
embroidered in leaves
drops to her heels.

Yunus said, "Paint her in your mind with your best metaphors and give the mural to the heart."

Will Yunus Nef'i's spirit return on one of Heaven's trains holding hands with Okwi? That would defy the rules of life and death. He neared the cliff of death, and she returned to the Better World. Heavenly people love with souls and do not kiss or hold hands. Her love for Yunus broke the sacred rules. Okwi, standing at the exit gate in the Other World and Yunus, does not mean their love story ended.

A native poet will show up one day with a pen and pad. He will write the story about Okwi, the charming lady, and Yunus, the old-bearded man. The theme will likely resemble Yunus' last story about a historical half of a rock tablet of Arabic inscriptions that the Native Chief, Umhagana, carried with her to Yemen. The rock, united with its missing half after being separated by 11 699 km for thousands of years, confirmed the two nations shared the same forebears.

War and grief discoloured the pupils of Yunus' eyes. Ageing shrunk his face. He always knew he could not go beyond his spiritual and physical means. On the border of death, with little wisdom left in a pulse, he lost half his sight and hearing. He put the present aside and placed his wishes in the hands of ALLAH. He pictured events he hoped to happen before or after his death. He shoved aside all thoughts coming in and out of his mind and wrote his wish list.

❦All U.S. hawks die of deep-rooted guilt—signs of the presidential race precipitate civil war white bigot against the other half of America. Erdogan mediates a peace treaty all signed. Obama and his family take refuge in

وَلاَ تَحْسَبَنَّ الَّذِينَ قُتِلُواْ فِي سَبِيلِ اللهِ أَمْوَاتًا بَلْ أَحْيَاء عِندَ رَبِّهِمْ يُرْزَقُون

Tehran. Jerad Kushner and his wife embraced Islam and moved to Turkey. The U.S. Lower and Upper Houses scrap the old face of America, adopt Turkey's laws, governing system, and constitution, and debate the future of Trump and Biden.

Four Arab dictators die in their sleep on the same night at the same time, tongues hanging from their mouths; eyes sitting in sockets like black rocks, blue blood blocking the ears; hands folded upward over the wrists; feet wrapped behind the body.

An Israeli tank chases a Palestinian child and collides with Netanyahu's bullet-proof car on Jabotinsky Street in Ramat Gan, within the metropolitan district of Tel Aviv. Netanyahu dies instantly. Torah Jews, the leftist party, and Palestinian mayors form a government, dismantle all settlements, and ask all Torah Jews and Palestinians living abroad, including all refugees, to return to Palestine.

Jaundice sweeps all Zionist clans living in Israel and elsewhere. World medical scientists identify unknown liver diseases eating away tissue by tissue of the whole body. They find no cure but confirm a prolonged gruelling death, like Sharon's eight years of feeding through a tube.

A thirteen-year-old refugee travels six hundred miles on foot; shoots Bashar between the eyes. Syrians refuse to bury the criminal. Moscow's mayor allows the burial near Red Square and Bashar's bronze statue to stand left to a copper donkey. Alawites and Shi'ites visit Red Square twice, kneeling before Bashar's statue, kissing the feet and saluting the copper donkey.

A Coptic woman kills Abdul Fattah Assisi in his bed and ties his wife to a rope. In the morning, she prepares the family breakfast, vacuums, and wipes surfaces in the guest and family rooms. The following day, she flees to Palestine and rents an apartment in a Palestinian-Jewish neighbourhood.

Ali Khamenei, his Mullahs, militias and Hassan Nasrallah, Nabih Beri and Michel Aoun all die of brain rapture caused by lies buildup, deception, murder, and defamation.

وَلَا تَحْسَبَنَّ الَّذِينَ قُتِلُواْ فِي سَبِيلِ الله أَمْوَاتًا بَلْ أَحْيَاء عِندَ رَبِّهِمْ يُرْزَقُونَ

❖An orphan from Grozny hides in the shower of the primary bathroom. He stabs Putin in the heart as Putin steps in for a pee. The orphan works as a gardener and a stud for Mrs. Putin. The Kremlin displayed Putin's red statue to the copper donkey's right and buried his rotten body beside Bashar.

❖Lightning hits Xi Jinping's bullet-proof limousine and reduces the president and vehicle to ashes.

❖Narendra Modi dies in his sleep with V.D. Savarkar's book "Essentials of Hindutva" on his chest. An autopsy shows Lichen Nitidus in his blood, a rare condition usually appears on the skin. Pathologists continue to investigate the cause.

❖Macron's wife leaves him for an ordinary man. He remarries an Algerian divorcee who poisons him on their honeymoon in Dubai for the same reason.

❖Boris develops muscular dystrophy and spends his time in a wheelchair.

❖Untruthful writers, journalists, poets, and thinkers, including Shi'ite and Sunni traitors, all die of a common disease known as the "sin and treason virus." Forensic doctors conclude the blood type belongs to the Iblis species.

❖The UN and the General Assembly collapsed and shut down all operations.

❖Turkish scientists invent an interceptor that neutralizes nuclear fumes and turns gases into harmless dust. Anchor a fleet of surveillance stations on several orbits. Deploy highly advanced submarines to break the code of the seven black boxes buried below the floors of the seven oceans.

The scientists conclude each box stores the origin and ecological changes of humans, animals, mammals, marine life, feathered theropod dinosaurs and the Jinn. Once they retrieve the first box, the other boxes will easily be recoverable. Turkey must find answers to seven world problems:

(1) Stop pollution. (2) Turn nuclear weapons into firecrackers. (3) Reform bigots into circuit monkeys and dictators into pigs in the image of a human

وَلاَ تَحْسَبَنَّ الَّذِينَ قُتِلُواْ فِي سَبِيلِ اللهِ أَمْوَاتًا بَلْ أَحْيَاء عِندَ رَبِهِمْ يُرْزَقُونَ

on two feet. (4) Turn over all state wealth and properties to Aoughaff Trust to manage. (5) Apply the justice system as prescribed in the Holy Qur'an to remedy and resolve all cases and issues between all humans, and all other species, including Nature. (6) Dismantle all Zionist settlements and dismantle the Zionist Lobby and all its chapters worldwide, return all stolen land and properties to Palestinians, and grant aboriginal status to all Torah Jews. Deport all Zionists to the country of their choice. (7) Release the Torah's original scriptures and the authentic Bible: One copy of each held in Turkey and the Vatican.

Yunus Nef'i died on December 31, 2019. The government of Canada flew his body to Yemen. The el-Hutaib villagers buried him at the highest hill of the village. Visit Yunus Nef'i's grave if you do not suffer from el-Hutaib's acrophobia of 10,000 feet elevation. Listen to the villagers' story about a star appearing in winter and sending squints of light when the clock strikes nine. Villagers say two angels carry an orb of clouds over the village as typical clouds in winter cannot float beyond eight thousand feet. Rain falls for two hours and stops. Snowflakes invade the skies and capture el-Hutaib in a white blanket. Yunus cannot see rain or snow, but flakes seep through the soil and touch his remains.

Professor of dignity, sharpen your sacred pen, catch thoughts as they rise like martyrs, hold them on paper mats. The wind will carry them to the Seven Skies. Egypt wrote her ode on the grieved clouds, painted you on a horse, wings attached to shoulders, tears in the eyes and an olive branch in hand. Palestine remembers your pen; her children recite your poems as they throw rocks at Israeli tanks. Despite scars growing deeper every tick of time, Syria, land, and sea mourn your departure.

Testify before your LORD Obama cold in heart and chest, emotion under feet: He watched barrels, submarine rockets, chemical weapons and missiles dice, shatter and mince all ages. Testify before your LORD Donald Trump and Zionist clans plan to seize el-Quds, Mecca, and Istanbul.

The sun misses your face, and the moon and the stars look for you every night. "Exile" failed to break you, change your skin, or sell you to a cut-and-paste West.

وَلاَ تَحْسَبَنَّ الَّذِينَ قُتِلُواْ فِي سَبِيلِ اللّهِ أَمْوَاتًا بَلْ أَحْيَاء عِندَ رَبِّهِمْ يُرْزَقُونَ

Encrypted messages in your prose and verse hide your inherent prophecies. Your critics often attacked your thoughts but could not remove one letter, shake word or line, bend, twist, or shudder the crystallized truth you raised from literary podiums in cafés and street corners.

Yunus Nef'i authored four books on Western injustices and seventeen poetry collections, including a dozen short stories and novels. He travelled to Africa and searched for Melaka for years. He went to Asia and the Middle East.

He lived in Sinai for several years and helped the survivors of the war. A helicopter's missile missed his door by several meters. His grandmother's stories built his passion for snowflakes as high as the el-Hutaib village. He first saw snow falling and landing when he and the small family arrived at the Port of Montreal on November 18, 1944.

ولاَ تَحْسَبَنَّ الَّذِينَ قُتِلُواْ فِي سَبِيلِ اللهِ أَمْوَاتًا بَلْ أَحْيَاء عِندَ رَبِّهِمْ يُرْزَقُونَ

154

ولاَ تَحْسَبَنَّ الَّذِينَ قُتِلُواْ فِي سَبِيلِ اللهِ أَمَوَاتًا بَلْ أَحْيَاء عِندَ رَبِّهِمْ يُرْزَقُونَ

Professor Yunus Nef'i
of Hutaib village, Yemen
August 31, 1930 – December 31, 2019

www.ingramcontent.com/pod-product-compliance
Lightning Source LLC
Chambersburg PA
CBHW050943050726
47592CB00007B/2414